Conversations with My Daughter

ROBERT VERES

iUniverse, Inc.
Bloomington

Conversations with My Daughter

iUniverse books may be ordered through booksellers or by contacting:

iUniverse
1663 Liberty Drive
Bloomington, IN 47403
www.iuniverse.com
1-800-Authors (1-800-288-4677)

Because of the dynamic nature of the Internet, any web addresses or links contained in this book may have changed since publication and may no longer be valid. The views expressed in this work are solely those of the author and do not necessarily reflect the views of the publisher, and the publisher hereby disclaims any responsibility for them.

Any people depicted in stock imagery provided by Thinkstock are models, and such images are being used for illustrative purposes only.

Certain stock imagery © Thinkstock.

ISBN: 978-1-4620-8374-9 (sc)
ISBN: 978-1-4620-8376-3 (e)
ISBN: 978-1-4620-8375-6 (dj)

Printed in the United States of America

iUniverse rev. date: 1/23/2012

This book is for Natalie, Audrey, Jesse, Anna, Moriah, and Patty, none of whom did anything even remotely like the things that you will read here.

Preface

"**D**addy, if you're really determined to write a book like this, don't you think you should write something at the start that explains what you're up to?"

"I'm not exactly sure what you mean by 'up to.'"

"People are going to want to know the purpose of the book. You're writing it for a reason, aren't you?"

"I'm going to raise the quality of parenthood around the globe in measurable ways. The needle will move visibly when this book is finally published."

"And why now? I mean, now that I'm grown and moved out of the house and married and all."

"You moved out? When?"

"Seven years ago."

"Now that you mention it, I did notice that your bedroom has been a lot less, less …"

"Messy?"

"I was actually going to say 'infested with all sorts of vermin,' but I suppose 'messy' is a more polite way to put it. And it *has* been a while since crude-looking misfits were knocking on the door, asking if you were ready for a date at the tattoo parlor. You remember that one who used to pick his teeth with the switchblade—"

"This is kind of what I was getting at. Shouldn't you explain the point of all this right up front? I mean, if you're going to be writing about my ex-boyfriends, you know, some of them are out on parole now and they might recognize who you're talking about."

"So really what you're hinting around about is you want me to explain to *you* what I'm, as you put it, 'up to.' Is that right?"

"Sort of, I guess. Yes."

"All right. If you really **must** know, I thought it would be beneficial for the human race as a whole if I captured some of the deep wisdom that I've applied to molding you into the fine, upstanding citizen that you've become today. I thought it would be a public service if I shared my examples with other parents who might be confused about how to, for example, respond to endless stalling when it's clearly time for their daughter to go to bed, *every single evening* for thirteen consecutive years. Or when their daughter suddenly decides to subsist on a nutritious diet consisting entirely of french fries, potato chips, and diet soda."

"That's an exaggeration. I never stopped liking candy."

"I'm going to capture for all posterity some of the truly inspirational things that I said to you, those wise sayings and observations that will stick with you and guide you forward through the turbulence of your adult years—"

"Please tell me you're kidding."

"—and that others will soon be able to seize on as beacons of insight in a dark and confusing world, where—"

"Daddy."

"What."

"Don't you actually have to **have** this wisdom thing before you start trying to write it down?"

"I'm not sure I see where you're going with this."

"I mean, all you ever did was fuss at me whenever I tried to wear anything more revealing than a nun's habit and try to scare away my boyfriends."

"That's not true. I also complained about the messiness of your bedroom, and on lots of occasions I made unflattering comments about your taste in music."

"And you were always trying to make me go to bed before the afternoon was half over. But I don't think any of that is what most people think of as excellent parenting skills."

"Your point being?"

"I'm just not sure people are going to be interested in taking advice from a parent whose daughter mostly remembers how he somehow got a court order against the high school to force them to beef up security so they could prevent her and every other girl from making out with their boyfriends in the art room and behind the cafeteria before homeroom started."

"Well—"

"I mean, how many fathers, *ever*, were so embarrassing at the mall that their daughter had a heart attack and had to be rushed to the emergency room?"

"The doctor said it was indigestion from eating so many french fries."

"Whatever. If people read this—this encyclopedia of wisdom, child-raising inspirational beacon of stuff parents should know—maybe what you ought to tell them, right up front, is that the true reality, at least as I remember it, is that you were always kind of clueless and sometimes way too uptight, but you were also a fun dad who clearly loved me in spite of a track record of appallingly bad parenting."

"You think that would inspire people to buy this book? If I wrote that in the first few pages, just like you said it?"

"It might propel your book all the way to blockbuster status."

"You really think so?"

"I'm absolutely sure of it."

"Wow. Okay. Hey, I really appreciate your advice here."

"Not a problem, Daddy. Just call me if you need anything else."

The Bedtime Ritual

Parental duties and responsibilities can seem overwhelming to the novice parent, and some psychological experts believe that daughters can, at times, be craftier and more complicated to raise than sons. The challenge of raising socially responsible children, in the midst of the many temptations to stray from the straight and narrow, has never been greater.

In this book, you'll find numerous examples of a firm, wise hand on the parenting tiller—actual parent–child dialogues that will help you understand exactly what to say when confronted with the many difficult or unexpected situations that you are likely to experience.

For example, in the early stages of your relationship with your daughter, she may occasionally attempt to assert her independence by testing your parental resolve. This testing activity will initially come to the surface during your daily bedtime ritual—a wonderful bonding time of intimacy where you will field occasional questions about whether your daughter can, perhaps, stretch the limits of her assigned time to go to sleep.

The wise parent demonstrates a firm and confident resolve, knowing that your daughter needs and appreciates clear boundaries in her life.

"For the thirty-eighth and final time, it's time for you to go upstairs to bed. Now."

"Please, can't I watch just one more show?"

"For the thirty-ninth and absolutely the final time, no. You've been stalling for the past three hours and seventeen minutes. If you give me any more trouble I'm going to do something drastic."

"Like what?"

"I'll—I'll light myself on fire and end it all right here."

"Cool! Right here in the living room? Can I please get the video camera out of the garage?"

"Absolutely not. It's time for bed, not for videotaping my last desperate attempt to get your attention."

"Just one show?"

"What show?"

"I think there's a cartoon movie marathon coming on."

"For the fortieth and final time—oh, the heck with it. Sure. Why not? Stay up all night if you want to. What do I care?"

[*Long pause.*]

"Why?"

"Why what?"

"Why are you letting me stay up all of a sudden?"

"Because I love you and want you to be happy."

"Come on. I know better than that."

"Because that way I can get some sleep for a change without having to read all those bedtime books about little bears and cats in a hat and saying good-bye to the moon."

"So I can watch TV?"

"That's right."

"And eat popcorn?"

"Don't push it."

"But I want somebody to read me a book. Could you, after the movie—"

"Not a chance."

"How about right now?"

"Will you come up to bed right now?"

"I want to get a drink first."

"Fine."

"And I have to go to the bathroom."

"I'll wait for you in bed."

"Do you think you could light yourself on fire anyway?"

"That depends on how long you spend in the bathroom."

Candy Tantrum

Nothing builds intimacy and mutual trust as efficiently as when the father and daughter take a quiet, relaxed, uneventful trip to the grocery store, sharing a common household chore. This may also, on occasion, provide a teachable moment where your little girl can learn about appropriate boundaries, and you can show the quiet strength and firmness that children ultimately crave from their loving parents.

"Is that everything on Mommy's grocery list?"

"Let's see. Eggs. Milk."

"Check."

"Toilet paper. Ewww."

"Check."

"Lettuce. Carrots. It said broccoli, but I crossed it off and put ice cream down instead."

"Good work. Check, check, and check."

"And candy."

"Wait a minute. Let me see that list."

"It said you should get me some of this candy on the way out. And gum."

"Didn't you get a candy bar the last time we were in here?"

"No."

"Isn't that a bold-faced lie?"

"I want some. Pleeaaase?"

"I curse whoever decided to put the candy and gum counter next to the checkout line in grocery stores. May he or she die of a horrible lingering illness—"

"Does that mean yes?"

"No."

"Does it mean maybe?"

"No. You had some last time. We aren't going to buy candy every time we go to the grocery store. By the time you're ten years old, you'll weigh a thousand pounds and have no teeth."

"I really, really, really want some. I do. I really do."

"Don't you want to grow up like one of these supermodels here? Look. I'll bet she never ate a candy bar in her whole life. She might not even have ever eaten a whole sandwich at once."

"You can't trick me. I want this one."

"Put it back. *Now.*"

"Which other one can I have then?"

"None. Look, we're almost at the front. Only … three more people in line ahead of us. One of the carts isn't even totally overflowing."

"Now! I want it now!"

Sigh.

"*Waaahhh!* Give it to me!"

"Honey, you know I'm only doing this for your own—"

Shriek. Wail. Holler. Scream. Bellow.

"Sir?"

"Yes."

"Excuse me, but your child seems to be unhappy about something."

"Really? I hadn't noticed."

"*Yaaaaaaaaaaahhhhhhhhh! Give it to me!*"

"Did you hit her or abuse her or something?"

"I certainly did not. We have a loving relationship."

"*Yowl!* I hate you! I hate you! I hate you!"

"Couldn't you be a good father and make her stop crying? It's moments like these that a young child needs love and comfort."

"You don't have kids of your own, do you?"

"Actually, no. How did you know?"

"*Yeeeeeowwwwwwwww! Bwah! Bwah! Bwah!*"

"Look, the strategy here is just to ignore her. When she realizes that I'm really, truly not going to give in, well, I'm hoping that will make her calm down."

"*Aaaaaaahhhhhhh!Aaaaarrrrrrghhh! Waaaaaawwwwwwwwhhhh!*" *Shriek!*

"Has that ever worked before?"

"No."

"*Aaaaiiiiiiiiyyyyeeeeeee! Yaaaaawwwwwwwww!*"

"What's the problem here?"

"His daughter is screaming her head off, and he claims he wasn't beating her."

"Do you believe him? I have a niece who works at the Department of Children's Services."

"*Yaaaaaaaaaagggggggghhhhhhh!*"

"She appears to be turning blue."

"Should we check her for bruises before you make the call?"

"All **right**! Okay. Honey. Darling. If I buy you this nice, thick piece of unhealthy chocolate, will you please stop screaming?"

"Yes, Daddy. Oh, I love you so much."

"See? She loves me. Are all of you satisfied now?"

"Well … are you sure it's healthy to be giving her all that candy?"

Showing and Telling

Starting with preschool or kindergarten, a child's world is suddenly divided into two entirely separate universes: the school and the home environment. The wise father will look for ways to bridge this gap and attempt, when the opportunity arises, to play a role in school activities.

One of the most surprising and enjoyable aspects of participating in your daughter's school life is gaining insight into the high esteem in which she holds you as she boasts about you to the little members of her peer group.

"Okay, darling, have a wonderful day at school."

"Aren't you coming in with me? You promised!"

"Promised what?"

"That I could take you to show-and-tell."

"That's today?"

"Yes. And you have to come."

"All right. Let me call work and tell them that I'm bedridden with a highly contagious disease, and we can walk in together and you can tell me what to do."

"Better make it quick. I don't want to be late."

"Okay, so where do I sit? These chairs are all kind of little. I'm not in preschool anymore."

"You can sit over there on the show-and-tell table next to Sarah's pet hamster and Johnny's laser death-ray rifle."

"Okay."

"Stop making faces at the other kids."

"Okay."

"Stop pretending to eat the hamster."

"Okay."

"Put the death-ray rifle down. Don't point it at the teacher."

"Okay."

"Just sit there."

"Okay."

"You can get up now. It's time for me to show-and-tell you."

"Okay."

"This is my daddy. He's my show-and-tell thing today, because I couldn't find my talking Elmo, which I think maybe I left at Carolyn Patterson's house last Tuesday."

"Can you tell the class something interesting about your daddy?"

"He's big and hairy."

"What kind of work does he do?"

"Nothing. He sleeps a lot. Sometimes I wish he was famous, like Barney the dinosaur or Thidwick the moose."

"Can you tell us what he does around the house?"

"He teases my mommy and holds me upside down when we go in the grocery store. Sometimes he's bad and I have to spank him."

"Does he play games with you?"

"No."

"Well, what do you like the most about him?"

"Sometimes when we play hide-and-seek, I'll go into my friend Catherine's house and play, and he spends all afternoon trying to find me."

"So *that's* where you were hiding all that time. That's not fair."

"It is too fair. You said I could hide anywhere."

"Um, what else can you tell us about your father?"

"I still say it was cheating."

"He says he works all day, but all I ever see him doing is sitting at the computer, wiggling his fingers around."

"It's called typing. It's very hard work. The amount of work I do in a day would exhaust whole herds of elephants."

"Be quiet. Show-and-tell things aren't supposed to talk."

"But you're—"

"Do you think your daddy works as hard as, say, a teacher does, keeping up with so many kids for hours every day?"

"Oh, no. Not even close."

"Do you think he makes more money than a teacher?"

"Well, he does have a nicer car than you do."

"Do you think that's fair?"

"No."

"Hey, wait a minute—"

"Maybe you could tell us one more thing about your daddy that the class would be interested in, and then we can have a nice visit with Sarah's hamster."

"Okay. Well … all right. You know how sometimes the daddy likes to pretend he's a monster, and he chases you around? Well, my daddy is the best monster, because he's old and slow and can't catch me, and he gets really tired whenever I run away, and I think he'll be even more fun when he gets really, *really* old, like next year when I'm five and I have longer legs."

"Okay. Now we can—"

"And I think he likes Johnny's gun, but he doesn't really like to eat hamsters."

Playing Cheerleader

The attentive father should always try to take time out from his important weekly activities to play games with his daughter. As he engages in this important developmental activity, his daughter will help him rediscover the simple pleasures of childhood activities and see his own adult world through fresh eyes.

"Daddy, what can I do?"

"What do you mean?"

"It's raining outside. There's nothing to do."

"You could clean your bedroom."

"Stop kidding around."

"Don't you have any friends you could play with?"

"No."

"How about your baby dolls?"

"They were all bad, so I made them take naps."

Sigh. "Do you want me to turn off this football game so you can watch one of your cartoon shows?"

"No. I want you to turn the TV off and play with me."

"Play what?"

"Cheerleader."

"What?"

"I'll be the cheerleader that tells everybody what to do, and you do the cheers with me, and we'll pretend the dog and cat are the people watching the game, and I'll teach you the cheers. Okay?"

"That doesn't sound like as much fun as watching this real,

actual football game. Plus, it sounds like I'll have to get up off of this couch."

"And jump up in the air and show team spirit and yell stuff."

"Can I be a very tired cheerleader and lay here on the couch?"

"Real cheerleaders don't do that."

"All right. The game's off. Now where do I stand?"

"Over here in front of the animals that are watching the game. Now do what I do. Yay! Team! Go!"

"Yay, team, go—"

"You don't have very much spirit."

"I told you I'm tired."

"Real cheerleaders aren't tired. Do it right, or I won't let you be on the cheerleading team."

"Really?"

"No."

"Okay, how's this? Go team, fight hard, and don't drop the ball or throw it to the wrong color uniforms or fall down when you're supposed to be tackling somebody and—you know, this is exactly what I say to the teams on the TV, except they never listen to me, for some reason …"

"That's not a cheer. Now do what I do. Yay! Team! Fight! Go! Team! Win! Break their bones! Spill their blood! Crush their—"

"Hold on a minute."

"You're not supposed to say, 'Hold on a minute.' You're supposed to do the cheer."

"But if you're going to be a cheerleader, you can't say those horrible things. That's what the fans are supposed to say. And the coaches."

"Oh. Okay, do this one. Give me an S!"

"S!"

"Give me a P!"

"P!"

"Give me an L!"

"L!"

"Give me an E!"

"E!"

"Give me a G!"

"G!"

"What does that spell?"

"Spleg? I don't think that's a word."

"You know I can't spell yet."

"Okay. Go Spleg! Fight! Win! Beat Glomph!"

"You're making fun of me."

"I'm trying to be a good cheerleader."

"If you don't do it right, I'm going to punish you."

"Don't let Glomph win!"

"Okay. I warned you."

"What are you going to do?"

"I'm going to make you take a horrible, terrible nap."

"No!"

"Yes. Lie down right there on the couch."

"Oh no! Have mercy! Like this?"

"Close your eyes."

"Okay. Like this?"

"Now don't move until I tell you to."

"I won't. I promise."

"Good. I'm going to wake up my baby dolls and tell them how bad you were."

Snore.

The Bad Student

*C*hildren thrive on role-playing and pretending, and it is always satisfying to your little girl when you participate in her world of imagination. Often your daughter will use this opportunity to reverse your roles and choose to play the authority figure.

This is your opportunity to set an example for your child and behave in your subservient capacity, exactly as you would want her to act when the game is over and you return to your position of authority.

"Let's play a game, Daddy."

"What kind of game?"

"School. I'll be the teacher and you can be the class."

"You aren't going to be a mean teacher, are you?"

"Just sit down and be quiet and do your work."

"What work?"

"I made up a worksheet for you."

"Teacher?"

"What?"

"This worksheet has a lot of hard things on it, like letters and numbers and things."

"You would know what letters and numbers are if you had been paying attention in class."

"Do I *have* to do this worksheet?"

"Yes. Or I'll make you sit in the corner."

"Teacher?"

"Yes?"

"I—I have to go to the bathroom."

"You just went."

"I did not! We just started playing."

"We're pretending you did."

"I have to go again."

"Sit down and do your work."

"But this work is too hard for me."

"Do it anyway."

"I think I'm going to cry."

"Do you want to stand in the corner?"

"No."

"Do you want me to spank your eyeballs with a stick?"

"**What!!?**"

"You're being a bad student."

"If you spank me, my daddy will come and bring his expensive trial lawyer and haul you to court, and you'll have to go to jail for a hundred years."

"We're pretending you don't have a daddy."

"Then I'll get my mommy to come down here."

"You don't have a mommy either."

"What *do* I have?"

"You have some work to do. Now get busy."

"If you'll let me go to the bathroom, I'll come right back. I promise."

"No you won't. You'll try to run upstairs like you did last time."

"Please?"

"No. Now be quiet and stop crying."

"That boy over there is hitting me. I'm going to throw my chair at him."

"Don't."

"That girl is bothering me. I'm going to take some scissors and cut off her ponytail."

"We're pretending that the other students are behaving and not bothering you."

"Could you pretend that I'm here while I go watch the football game?"

"No."

"I'm going to go to the bathroom anyway."

"Do you want me to get my whip?"

"Your *what*?"

"It's a special teacher whip. For bad students."

"I'm a very good student."

"Sometimes you are."

"*Now* can I go to the bathroom?"

"Let's pretend that it's time to spank the bad student."

Old Age

Young girls are naturally curious about the aging process, and of course it is difficult for their young minds to achieve perspective on the subtle shades of maturity in the adult population. When questioned about your age and the age of others in your daughter's orbit, you should endeavor to provide clarity and help address the inevitable confusion about the passage of years.

"Daddy, how old are you?"
"Honey, why do you want to know that?"
"I made a bet with Angelina."
"What kind of bet?"
"She said you were older than her grandpa. Are you, Daddy?"
"Certainly not. I'm forty-one."
"Wow!"
"What do you mean, 'wow'?"
"That's really old. Are you sure—"
"Yes. I'm in the prime of life."
"Was television invented when you were little?"
"It was invented, but my dad was too cheap to—"
"Did they have cars back then?"
"Mostly we just squatted around in caves. It was very cold, until one day somebody invented fire. It was better after that."
"Gosh! Did you work on the pyramids?"
"Only the big one."
"What was it like in the olden days?"

"Just like now, except we kids went out and played in the backyard instead of a soccer league with coaches and referees and travel schedules that take eight-year-old girls into entirely different states."

"It sounds boring."

"We didn't know any better, I guess."

"Will I ever be as old as you?"

"I hope so. Then you won't think it's so old. And I'll be seventy-four years old then."

"Whoa! Is that the oldest anybody has ever been?"

"Your grandmother is older than that right now."

"Wow! I'll bet she played with dinosaurs when *she* was little."

"I think that would be a great question to ask her."

"Do you like being old?"

"It depends. I don't have a bedtime, like you do, and I get to drive a car. But it isn't as much fun when I'm playing chasing games with you and your friends, and you're all too fast and tricky for me to catch you."

"I'm sorry."

"If you're so sorry, why did you just giggle?"

"I was just … thinking of something funny. That's all."

"You *like* it that I'm old and slow. Look, you're giggling right now."

"I"—*giggle*—"am not."

"I'm going to give you something to giggle about, young lady. I'm going to tickle you. Hey, come back here!"

Giggle.

"I see you behind that tree. If you weren't so darned fast—"

Giggle.

Dangerous Rescue

Younger children are naturally compassionate and giving, and the responsible parent will want to encourage these positive characteristics. The best opportunities come on that inevitable day when your child enlists your aid in caring for an injured or helpless animal.

"Daddy, look what I found!"

"Good Lord in heaven, what the hell is that?"

"Marilyn's daddy said it's a full-grown ocelot. He said to get it off his property or he'd get a court order. Daddy, what's a court order?"

"It seems to be unconscious. Where did you find it?"

"In the middle of the six-lane highway, about two miles from here."

"*What!* What were you doing in the middle of the highway? How many times have I told you—"

"Is it going to be all right?"

"I'm wondering what it's going to do when it wakes up. It must weigh fifty pounds."

"I'm afraid it might be hurt."

"If it's hungry, it might decide to get a quick lunch by eating one of us. After that—"

"Can we keep it, Daddy? I'll take care of it. I promise I will."

"Honey, it's a wild animal. It will tear up our house, bite and scratch us, invite other ocelots into our living room, and poop all over the carpet, in between the blood stains. Your mother will be really angry when she visits us in the emergency room."

"Please?"

"Help me get it into the dog cage. We'll take it to the vet and see what she suggests we do."

"*Then* can we keep it?"

"Quick, before it wakes up and gets annoyed."

"Are we almost there, Daddy?"

"This is the parking lot. I think it might be waking up."

Shriek! Wail! Hiss!

"Carry it gently, Daddy. You're bouncing it all around."

"I don't"—*grunt*—"think it's very"—*gasp*—"happy in there. Open that"—*grunt, gasp*—"door for me, will you?"

Shriek! Wail! Howl!

"Sir, your pet sounds a bit agitated. It's scaring those pit bulls over there."

"It's not"—*grunt*—"our pet. We think it may be"—*gasp, wheeze*—"an ocelot."

"Good Lord in heaven. And you brought it *here?*"

"Yes. I thought maybe—"

"I found it. We think it may be hurt. Can you please, please, please make it all better?"

Growl! Hiss!

"I'm not about to try to examine whatever you have in there. Unless you're willing to take it out of that container and pacify it—"

"With what? A taser?"

"Don't take that tone of voice with me—"

Moan! Growl!

"*Now* look what you've done. The pit bulls are wetting the floor."

"What *I've* done? All I did was—honey, what are you—no! Stop! It's going to—"

"My god, what *is* that thing?"

"Darling, put that thing down right now before it eats a pit bull and I have to pay—"

Purr. Lick.

"Look, Daddy. It's purring. I think it just wanted to be out of the carrier."

"Isn't that cute. Maybe a little scratch behind the—"

Growl! Snarl!

"Sir, I'd be careful about approaching that thing. Let me have a look. Maybe a broken rib or two ... the legs and hindquarters appear to be intact. Can you turn it this way, little girl?"

Purr.

"I think you can safely return it to the wild. I'd do it quickly, before it gets hungry."

"Can't we keep it?"

"Not if you value your life. It's showing an unhealthy interest in those two cowering pit bulls. Maybe it would be safer if you took this conversation outside."

"Honey, do you think you could put it back inside—"

"Daddy, he doesn't like it in there."

"She."

"What?"

"She appears to be pregnant. Now if you could get her safely on the other side of the front door—"

"Daddy, did you hear that? Fluffy is going to have babies."

"Fluffy?"

"We have to give her a name."

"Just get in the car and try not to let that ... to let *Fluffy* get too agitated."

"Are we going home?"

"We're going to the woods on the other side of that dangerous highway that you should never even *look* at again, and put that ... put *Fluffy* where she can find the nice daddy cat, who's probably so worried about her and the new babies that he's clawed down an oak tree."

"You're just making that up so I won't feel bad."

"Did it work?"

"Sort of. I'll miss you, Fluffy. I wish you could stay with us."

Purr.

"Daddy?"

"Yes, darling?"

"Someday, could we go visit Fluffy?"

"Yes."

"Really? I thought you were going to say no."

"In fact, we can make the first visit this afternoon."

"Today?"

"We'll carry Fluffy far enough into the woods so she's safely away from the highway. Then I figure it will take a while for those ribs to heal, and there might not be a delicious family pet in easy hunting distance. So we'll go to the store and get a few pounds of ground beef and come back and leave it in the woods near where we dropped her off."

"Can we get cat food instead?"

"Maybe some tuna fish, while we're at it."

Purr.

"It might take days for the ribs to heal. Can we come back and do it again?"

"If you'll remind me, we'll go back this weekend and see if she's eaten the food we dropped off. If she did, we'll leave more."

"Goody. So, Daddy?"

"Yes."

"I know I can't keep Fluffy."

"I'm glad you understand."

"I totally understand. She's a wild animal."

"Right."

"But, Daddy—"

"What?"

"When she has kittens, do you think one of them might need a good home?"

A Special Drink

*C*hildren excel in creativity; they can be creative in ways that will surprise and challenge the more rigid adult mind. Whenever you encounter examples of your daughter's creative thinking, remember to be supportive and encouraging.

"Here, Daddy. Drink this."

"What is it?"

"Try it. I made it myself."

"Aaaaaghhh!. What in god's name *is* this?"

"A little bit of orange juice and ketchup, and sugar and flour, and chocolate syrup and vinegar, and some stuff I found under the kitchen sink. It's my own special recipe. I made it just for you."

"How cute."

"When you finish it, I'll make another one."

"I'm not actually very thirsty right now. Can I put it here next to me and drink it all down when I get thirsty?"

"No."

"How about if we *pretend* that I'm drinking it. See? Look."

"That's not very good pretending. Don't you like it?"

"Do you want me to be honest?"

"No. I want you to tell me you like it and drink it all down so I can make a really big giant one for you using one of Mom's flower vases, and you can like that one too."

"I'm not sure I'd survive. Why don't you go tell your mom what you made, ask her if she wants one, and I'm pretty sure I'll have this finished by the time you get back."

"Okay, Daddy."

"But you can't make another one. We might run out of all these ingredients, and then your mom can't cook."

"Should I tell her that too?"

"Yes."

"Anything else?"

"Yes. Tell her how you made this, and say that if she wants a drink, she can't have it, because I'm finishing every drop. That will probably make her cry."

"I don't want her to cry."

"Too bad. Now hurry up. I have to go in the kitchen and get something out of the refrigerator."

"Do you really think Mommy will cry?"

"I think you should go find out."

"Okay. But … do you mind if I give the special drink to *her* instead? You've already had a taste. Don't look sad. It's okay."

"Well … okay. I don't want your mom to cry either."

"Goody. Thanks, Daddy."

"You're welcome, darling."

"Doesn't it feel good to be nice?"

"Yes. Yes, it does."

Psychology at Work

A respectful father–daughter relationship is built on the solid foundation of functional communication. Yet there may be those occasional times when the dialogue becomes inappropriately emotional or heated or punctuated by raised voices. The parent should immediately recognize that, on these occasions, the emotional context of the conversation is interfering with efficient communication. This may be a propitious time to discover the powerful communication benefits of applied child psychology.

"Daddy, why is the sky always blue?"

"Yes, dear."

"Yes what?"

"Hmmmm?"

"You weren't even listening to me. You think that book is more important than satisfying my unquenchable preadolescent thirst for knowledge."

"I do not."

"Do too!"

"Do not!"

"Do too!"

"As it happens, this book is about you, and me, and our relationship. It was written by a clinical psychologist who can help us communicate better."

"Does he have kids?"

"That's funny, your mother asked the same question. As it turns out, he's a lifelong bachelor with no kids of his own. But he has a lot of knowledge and wisdom and expertise, and he's giving me a lot of great advice on how to avoid having so many of our conversations deteriorate into childish fights."

"We don't get into childish fights when we talk."

"Yes we do."

"Do not!"

"Do too!"

"Do not!"

"Do too!"

"Quit screaming at me! I hate you when you scream at me!"

"You screamed first!"

"Did not!"

"Did too!"

"Did not!"

"Anyway, this is about active listening and demonstrating to you that I'm really hearing what you're saying. It's pretty good stuff. I'm going to use some of the techniques whenever we talk from now on. In fact, it suddenly occurs to me that we're talking right now."

"What kind of techniques?"

"Don't sound so suspicious. One of them is reflecting back what you say in exactly the way you said it. It reassures you that I heard you, and that I was listening, and that I cared about what you said."

"Whatever. I just wanted to ask you a question."

"I hear you saying that you wanted to ask me a question."

"Um, right. Didn't I just say that?"

"Now you're wondering whether you said what you were saying earlier."

"No, I wasn't."

"You were too."

"No!"

"Yes!"

"Are you going to answer my question or not?"

"What question?"

"Don't shout at me!"

"I'm—that is, now you're asking me not to shout at you."

"I sure as hell am."

"Don't you use that word around me, young lady."

"*You* use it."

"Do not!"

"Do too!"

"I'm going to go back to reading my book."

"Can't you answer my question first? I wanted to know why the sky is blue."

"Now you're telling me that you are interested in knowing why the sky is blue."

"Right. So why is it?"

"Now you're continuing to express your youthful curiosity."

"You don't know, do you?"

"You're saying that you don't believe I know the answer to your original question."

"Actually, I think you have no clue, and you're just trying to annoy me until I go away."

"I am not!"

"You are too!"

"Am not!"

"Are too!"

"Am not!"

"Are too!"

"Am not!"

"Are too!"

The Bedtime Ritual Revisited

Perhaps no other aspect of a father–daughter relationship leads to more intimacy and conflict than the ritual of preparing to go to sleep at night.

Earlier, we saw one example of how to maintain appropriate bedtime boundaries when your child is trying to overstep them. But as the years pass, you'll discover that the bedtime ritual will grow more complex, interesting, and challenging.

"Honey, turn off the TV. It's time for bed."

"Already?"

"It's past your bedtime. You said if I let you watch one more movie, you'd go to bed without any squawking or protest or stalling or any of your usual tricks."

"I don't think it's really my bedtime yet."

"It's four in the morning."

"Carolyn gets to stay up until five in the morning."

"Carolyn's parents are obviously idiots."

"You never let me do anything. And anyway, I'm not tired."

"You are too. You can hardly keep your eyes open."

"Can't I just watch one more movie? A short one?"

"No. Absolutely not. Now pick out eight or nine books and come upstairs to bed."

"I want ten books."

"All right, ten then."

"Can I have this one?"

"That's a telephone book."

"That's what I want."

"It's very boring."

"I don't care. And this one?"

"That's the unabridged dictionary."

"Please?"

"I think you're just stalling."

"You always say that."

"That's because you're always stalling. Now come upstairs to bed right now."

"Can I get a drink of water?"

Sigh. "Yes. But hurry."

"Can I get two drinks?"

"No. Now hurry up."

"I also have to go to the bathroom."

"No. Absolutely not."

"Please?"

Sigh. "Just be quick about it. And don't take too long changing into your nightclothes."

"Okay, Daddy."

"Well?"

"Well what?"

"*Go.* Get your drink. Get moving."

"I'm thinking about what I want."

"All right, I'm not reading any books."

"I'm going. You don't have to be so grumpy about it. Why are you always so grumpy about everything?"

"Maybe it's the lack of sleep."

"Well, next time sleep more so we don't have to get all fussy about me getting a drink before I go to bed."

"How can I sleep when you're keeping me up *right now*?"

"Maybe you could go to bed early, and I could wake you up when I'm ready to go to sleep so you could read to me *and* get a decent night's sleep."

"Would you do that?"

"Sure, if you gave me more allowance."

"How much?"

"Don't look so suspicious. Eighteen more dollars a week."

"Five."

"Eleven."

"Seven fifty."

"Twelve."

"Deal. Now turn that TV back on while I put this dictionary away and get some sleep."

"Okay, Daddy. I'm hurrying."

"Good."

Career Anxiety

Your preteen daughter is a blank slate waiting to be filled by experience and a lifetime of decisions. But there will be times when she will look at her life and wonder whether it will ever come to fulfillment in the way she sees that it has with the adults in her life.

Taking pages from your own life experience, you can reassure her that this existential insecurity is entirely normal, and use this opportunity to help her create a framework for setting realistic goals for her own bright and optimistic future.

"Daddy, when you were my age, did you ever worry about where your life was going?"

"You mean, was I afraid I was going to fail fifth grade for the third time and never make it out of elementary school?"

"No, that's not—"

"Or that someday I'd apply for a job and discover that it was on my permanent record that I cut that little girl's pigtail off in class?"

"You really did that?"

"As far as I know, no written record of it has survived. I'm waiting for the statute of limitations to run out."

"Does that mean yes?"

"Maybe this would be a good time to tell me what you're so worried about in this interestingly adult way."

"I can't figure out what I want to be when I grow up."

"That's not really a problem at your age. I don't think they make you commit to a definitive career path until you're twelve or thirteen."

"But everybody else seems to know exactly what they want to be."

"Like who?"

"Cindy Nelson wants to be a Dallas Cowboys cheerleader and wiggle her butt in front of millions of fans. Tommy Watson wants to be a double agent and betray two global superpowers at the same time. Emily Nickerson wants to be like her dad and work on Wall Street and screw people out of their money."

"Those are very ambitious goals."

"And I don't know *what* I want to be. I want to be important and famous and boss people around and have enough money to buy all that cool stuff that you're always telling me we can't afford without taking out a second, third, and fourth mortgage on the house. I want to sail my own cruise ship around my own tropical island. I just don't know what kind of work I want to do to get there. Should I be a fireman? Or a schoolteacher? Or a drug lord? Or a bank teller? It seems like there are too many choices to just pick one."

"Maybe you need a hero."

"A what?"

"A hero is nothing more than somebody you really respect and admire. When I was a kid, there was Roy Rogers, the cowboy who always got the better of the bad rustlers and horse thieves, and then he would sing a song about it. It never took him more than an hour or two."

"You want me to be a horse thief?"

"No, you're missing the concept. There was Bob Cousy, the great basketball player whose heart was so big it made up for the fact that he was half the size of a midget. Or Willie Mays, who played baseball exactly the way I did in Little League, except that he could hit the ball past second base and catch the ball with his glove instead of the back of his head, and when he threw it to the infield, it would never sail off and clobber any of the fans in the wooden bleachers behind first base. You'd pick somebody who was all the things you wanted to be, and that kind of gave you a sense of direction while you grew into whomever you were destined to become."

"How do I find somebody like that?"

"Well, you might consider your very own father as a kind of hero to follow and emulate."

"Oh, Daddy, you're so funny sometimes."

"Well, let's look around for a minute. You could pick a famous actress with unimpeachable virtue, who, despite being so shockingly beautiful, would never think of stealing somebody else's husband on the set or 'accidentally' releasing a nasty video of —well, I can't really think of anybody like that right now. Maybe a politician who puts principle and the good of the country before fund-raising and pandering to special interests and getting elected—okay, maybe that's not realistic either. A professional athlete who dignifies the sport and would never even consider taking performance-enhancing—gosh, this is harder than I thought."

"Could I be a welfare mom who pretends to have a lot of kids?"

"I'd rather you chose a career path that doesn't routinely violate any federal or state laws."

"How about a professional kickboxer?"

"Maybe, for now, we can just say that you're waiting to find yourself, and you're temporarily living with your parents until you have it figured out. Then people will think you're in your late twenties."

"I guess I don't have to make a final decision just yet."

"There really is plenty of time."

"And meanwhile, I could practice trying out new things and see if I like them."

"You actually could."

"Could I borrow some of the kitchen knives for the afternoon?"

"I guess so, so long as you bring them back in good shape."

"I promise. I'm just taking them to creepy Brian Houser's place for a few hours. He's that boy who likes to catch and eat lizards, just to gross everybody out. I think there must be something seriously wrong with him."

"Just—you know—to satisfy my curiosity, what potential career option are you thinking about practicing first?"

"Brain surgery."

Problems at School

It's not always easy for your child to understand the long-term importance of fully engaging her mind in the classroom and taking advantage of an educational system that offers, essentially free of charge, a chance to learn all the amazing information that the human race has accumulated in the last ten thousand years.

One of your most important obligations as a parent is to closely monitor your child's daily progress at school and to help her make subtle course corrections whenever her commitment to learning begins to waver.

"Honey, your report card came in the mail today. Do you have time to talk to me about it?"

"Not today, Daddy. I'm updating my Facebook page and looking at funny YouTube videos."

"I thought you were going to say you were too busy doing your homework."

"I've already come up with my excuse for tomorrow."

"This will only take a second. I wanted to ask you about this note that your principal sent me about you."

"What does he want now?"

"He says that you were misbehaving in class."

"That's a total lie!"

"He was pretty specific. Did you actually spit on your teacher?"

"She was trying to bring me inside from recess so I could take some stupid test. I told her to leave me alone. What else was I supposed to do?"

"It says here that you pulled a switchblade on one of the serving women in the lunchroom. Where did you even *get* a switchblade?"

"Same place I got the stiletto. There's a creepy guy who hangs around the edge of school grounds and sells drugs to the second graders."

"Let's see what else it says here. Throwing chairs at the other students ... biting the music teacher ... inciting riots on the playground ... starting fires in the lavatory using history textbooks as kindling ... and it says you haven't turned in a single homework assignment since the middle of October. I wonder why they're only now telling me this in February."

"He has such an imagination."

"Which brings me to the subject of your grades. I did notice that you managed to pull your English grade up to a D-, but the rest of these grades are awful. I didn't know they even gave out grades lower than an F."

"I *thought* I might have gotten one of those questions right on the English midterm, but I was too busy texting to be sure. Do you know how hard it is to concentrate on your texting when the teacher is droning on and on and on?"

"Listen, honey, we need to have a talk about priorities and appropriate behavior, and you need to give me that switchblade before it gets you into any more trouble."

"Okay, Daddy. But be careful with it. It's awfully sharp, and I think David Weatherby's blood is still on it, so it's probably crawling with cooties."

"See, the reason we send you to school is so you can learn things. Stuff like how to multiply, and who was the father of our country, and proper grammar, so that when you grow up, if you get a really good education and go to college, someday you can help your own kids with *their* homework."

"I never realized how important it was."

"And you need to show respect to the school officials, and be courteous to the other students."

"Even if they annoy me?"

"It's an important life lesson. Someday you'll have a boss who will annoy you, and your cubicle will be surrounded by backbiting coworkers, and your desk will be filled with meaningless paperwork that has no relation to the real world, and you can't just go around spitting on them or carving them up like an oven-basted turkey or setting the building on fire. You might get fired, and then the government will give you unemployment insurance to sit around and watch TV in your underwear until the checks stop coming, after which you'll have to claim welfare payments, because the job market is too tight for people to be hiring dangerous psychopaths. You don't want that, do you?"

"I guess not. Is it really that bad at your office?"

"Worse."

"You know, Daddy, maybe you could, you know, rebel a little bit. Keep them off balance. It's been working great for me."

"What do you mean?"

"When I walk down the halls, some of the teachers go clear over to the other side of the hallway and hope I won't notice them. Once a whole sixth-grade class was walking in line to the lunchroom, but when they saw me, they turned around and scattered back to their classroom."

"You think something like that would make everybody leave me alone at work?"

"You'll have to put some effort into it. But now that you have that switchblade—"

"And I guess I could get a lighter. Or would matches be better?"

"I prefer matches, but that's really a personal decision."

"I'm not real good at spitting."

"It takes practice."

"Thanks, honey. I'm glad we had this talk. I think I really learned something today."

"Think nothing of it. That's what I'm here for."

Standing Your Ground

How does the wise parent stand his ground when his daughter makes unreasonable requests? The key is to anchor the discussion in logical arguments supported by the facts. You might be tempted to weigh your daughter's disappointment too heavily in the decision equation; if so, try to remember how resilient she is. Chances are, as intense as it may be now, the entire discussion will be forgotten by tomorrow morning.

"Daddy, can I have a dog?"

"Certainly not. Dogs carry fleas, and they bark at all hours of the night. And they might bite you."

"You never let me have anything!"

"How can you say that? Didn't I let you take violin lessons when you were seven?"

"You *made* me do that. I *hated* violin lessons."

"Really? I thought you loved them."

"I told you eleven thousand million times that I hated to practice. Why do you think I dropped the violin off the roof?"

"You did that *deliberately*? That instrument cost more than five hundred dollars!"

"A dog wouldn't cost that much."

"Besides, who would take care of it?"

"I would."

"Just like you took care of your pet hamster?"

"That wasn't my fault. It only got sick after Alyssa dressed it up in baby clothes and fed it peanut butter, goat cheese, and toilet bowl cleaner."

"And that's another thing—who would feed this dog every morning and night? Who would make sure it has water?"

"I would."

"Right."

"I *would*."

"Just like you clean your room?"

"The roach problem in my room is completely gone."

"Only because we called in the exterminator. Remember? He wouldn't cross the threshold at first because he said it was a fire hazard. Besides, who would walk this dog whenever it needs to go to the bathroom?"

"Ew."

"Sometimes you have to give a dog a bath."

"I *love* giving baths. I could use my new shampoo."

"You will not. That shampoo costs more per ounce than enriched uranium. Why don't you wait fifteen or twenty years until you're a responsible adult and then get a dog that you can take proper care of?"

"I want one *now*. Please? Pretty please?"

"Absolutely not."

"Pretty, *pretty* please?"

"This conversation is over."

"With sugar on top?"

"Real sugar, or that fake stuff your mom makes me use in my coffee?"

"Real. And chocolate."

"Chocolate on top too?"

"And that kind of beer you like so much."

"Hmmmm."

"And a nice, ripe strawberry."

"All right. Okay. Fine. Tomorrow, we'll go to the dog shelter and look for some poor, abandoned mongrel whose life has been so sad that it will actually *enjoy* being dressed up in baby clothes, and—"

"Oh, Daddy, you're so wonderful. But you don't have to go to all that trouble."

"What do you mean?"

"Alison! Alison! It's okay! You can bring the dog inside! He said yes!"

"Oh my god, I can't believe you talked him into it. How did you do it?"

"I just used the 'pretty please' thing on him again and kept adding things. It wasn't hard at all, really."

"Girls—"

"You are *so* lucky. My dad would never fall for something that stupid."

"Girls, I—"

"What are you going to call it?"

"*Girls!* Listen to me! *Now!*"

"Yes, Daddy."

"Yes, sir."

"This, this *creature* appears to weigh more than two hundred pounds, and from the way it's backed me into a corner, I think it might have the idea that I'm not the lord and master of this house but part of the food supply."

"Oh, sorry, Daddy. Come here, Foofy. That's a good dog. I think if we give him some real food, he'll stop trying to eat you, and that will be a good way to remind us to keep his bowl full every day, don't you think?"

"Do you have any idea how much a creature like that eats?"

"We already know. That's why Johnny's mom and dad said they couldn't keep him. They said after two days he was costing them more than the car payments."

"That's exactly what I—"

"So they gave us six bags of dog food to go with him. It should last him at least until morning."

"Well—"

"I'll take him upstairs and give him a bath, just like you said."

"Use your *mother's* shampoo."

"Okay, Daddy. Come on, Alison. After we give Foofy a bath, we can go outside and see if we can find another stray animal that can be Foofy's little brother or sister."

A Firm Refusal

It is not uncommon for a daughter of any age to ask for gifts that are either unaffordable or age-inappropriate. To set appropriate gift expectations, start by gently exploring the reasons behind the request that you intend to deny, and then smoothly redirect your daughter's interest toward a similar gift that would be less expensive and more suitable.

"Honey, what would you like for your birthday this year?"

"Well, I was hoping for a new car."

"A toy automobile! What a cute idea."

"Actually, I was thinking of the kind you see on the highways. A Porsche, one of those little two-seaters with the six hundred–liter engine and big speakers so I can crank up my gangsta rap albums at thirty-five miles an hour over the speed limit."

"Whatever gave you the idea that we could afford something like that? Even if we thought it was appropriate for you, which I definitely do not."

"You don't have to spend your own money on it. I'll ask Grandma."

"Grandma wouldn't think of giving working, high-performance automobiles to eleven-year-old girls."

"That's no fair! If I'm old enough to drink and have sex, I certainly ought to be able to drive."

"There are state and federal laws involved here. And—wait a minute. What was that thing you said about—"

"All you'd have to pay for is the gas and the accident repair."

"Maybe we should focus our attention on something a little more reasonable. How about a nice baby doll?"

"Can you buy me a motorcycle?"

"What could you possibly do with a motorcycle?"

"Go out joyriding on the freeway."

"Don't you think that's a pretty dangerous thing to do?"

"I guess so."

"Please don't start crying. I'm trying to do what's best for you. When you've lived as long as I have, you can see that some things are just too dangerous for an eleven-year-old to be allowed to do. I don't expect you to understand this at your age, but someday you'll thank me for it."

"Yes, Daddy."

"Besides, motorcycles and automobiles are pretty expensive."

"A lot more than bicycles."

"That's right. You can get a really nice bike for three hundred dollars. A decent motorcycle runs in the thousands, and I'd probably have to trade this house for the car you wanted."

"I guess you get more exercise riding a bicycle."

"That's another good point."

"And you'll probably tell me a bike is a lot safer."

"Yes, I will."

"I wish the bike I have now wasn't too small for me. I'd probably be able to get by without a motorcycle or a high-performance sports car if I just had a new bike."

"That's good thinking. You know, we could probably get to the bike shop before it closes and take a look around, and maybe you could show me something that would be appropriate for your birthday."

"If you think that's best. After all, you are a lot older and wiser than I am."

"Yes. And don't you ever forget it."

48

Selecting Boyfriends

As a parent, you may be dreading the day when your daughter begins dating. Try to recognize this as your first opportunity to help her refine her selection criteria.

"Hi, darling. What are you looking at? It looks like a lot of pictures of boys."

"It's a preteen dating site. There just aren't any interesting men in my junior high school, so this expands my dating pool."

"Now I'm curious. What do they say on there?"

"I've picked out some of the more interesting ones. Look at him. Isn't he hot?"

"He looks like he's in his thirties. Is that a switchblade in his hand?"

"He might have gotten left back a few times. Look at his profile."

[*Reading.*] "Dangerous misfit with a violent criminal record looking for young innocent chick who likes bad boys. Sexual experience preferred but not necessary. My god in heaven—"

"He's cute, but he still lives with his mother. Here's another one: [*reading*] Steaming hot jock with a knack for knocking up girlfriends, looking for innocent young babe with a great body and large, firm knockers who wants to lose the stigma of her purity. I enjoy long walks on the beach until it gets too dark for the cops to find us nestled together up in the sand dunes in a disorderly pile of our own clothing. Daddy, doesn't he sound romantic?"

"He sounds totally unacceptable. Here, let me see if I can find the local police website. Or do you have some kind of phone app that will make it easier to alert the federal authorities about this dangerous misfit?"

"Here's a nice boy who was arrested for assaulting an entire nursing home. Or—"

"Wait. Scroll back a minute. There, look at that one. *He* might be somebody worth considering."

[*Reading.*] "Honor roll student who hasn't reached puberty yet, looking for scripture-reading partner. I enjoy chess, reading ahead in my school textbooks, French club, and religious fellowship meetings. Hobbies include stamp collecting and tending my mutual fund portfolio. Copies of my chastity pledge available upon request. Daddy, don't you think he's a little too … *boring* for me?"

"I think you should give him a try. I'll bet he's a really good handholder."

"You think so?"

"Definitely."

New Phone

Comparing notes on the latest communication technology with a teenage girl can be a humbling experience for the tech-challenged members of an older generation. It is also a chance to get educated and to use this information to make parental judgments about appropriate expenditure boundaries.

"Daddy, I really need a new phone."

"What's wrong with the one you have?"

"It's old and it won't do anything."

"Like what?"

"Take holograph movies of my friends and me. Track satellites. Do my homework while I'm watching reality shows."

"You know, when I was your age, telephones had a really, *really* cool app that I don't hear much about anymore."

"What?"

"It was really cool. You could input a specific set of numbers into the device, and then you could talk to just about anybody you wanted to, live."

"Oh, Daddy—"

"Take a look at my phone. It does everything I need it to."

"Yeah. Okay, suppose you want to text your friends about, you know, like somebody has a really good price on designer jeans or marijuana or something. What do you do then?"

"Aha! I expected that question. Look here. You push this button here, and presto! Out pops a tiny little hammer and chisel. You can use the hammer and chisel to create your message on this piece of stone here."

"Yeah. And it uses the cuneiform operating system."

"Is that bad?"

"They talk about it in my history books, either right before or after the Vietnam War and Charlemagne and all those other ancient historical things they force us to learn about. It's very old."

"Okay. All right. How much is this new phone going to cost?"

"If you sign up for the plan where you get unlimited Internet access and you've prepaid so I can download any movies I want and you sign up for automatic Twitter alerts from all the reality TV people, which costs more if they're sending naked pictures from prison, then it's only six hundred dollars with the mail-in rebate. My friend Janine just got one. She's the one who just joined that motorcycle gang. In fact, she's texting me now, from somewhere in Montana, it looks like ..."

"Are you sure you *need* this, or just want it?"

"Daddy, you ask the most ridiculous questions ..."

The Untidy Bedroom

Probably since humans squatted in caves, young girls have craved not only their own space, but some measure of control over it. For many daughters, the bedroom is gradually transformed from a convenient place to sleep to a sanctuary of personal space, and, at times, the room may seem untidy to the parental eye.

This is your opportunity to teach your daughter the importance of good organizational skills and help her set high standards of cleanliness that will eventually carry over into the way she maintains her own home some years down the road.

"Bye, Daddy. I'll be back in a couple of hours."

"Hold on a minute. Did you clean your room like I asked you?"

"Yes, Daddy."

"Let's take a look."

"*No!* I mean, I'm kind of in a hurry."

"I just want to see it before you go."

"Couldn't I just—"

"What's that smell?"

"Don't open that—"

"Oh, my god. What happened in here? It looks like three or four tornadoes played tag in your bedroom. What *is* that smell?"

"I'm sure it's nothing. I—"

"Maybe you and I have a different definition of a clean bedroom, young lady, but *my* definition doesn't include sedimentary layers of clothing so deep that the lower layers are starting to decompose, and you could have at least picked the dresser back up off the floor and put the drawers back into it. And how many plates of rotting food do you have scattered around in here? Seven, eight, nine, ten—maybe you should start eating in the dining room with the rest of us."

"*Now* can I go?"

"Are you kidding? You haven't even *started* cleaning up in here. Before you leave the house, I want every piece of clothing to be washed and hung up in its proper place in the closet. I want these hangers to be put away, the dresser stood upright with the drawers in place and filled with folded underwear and sorted socks, the plates, dishes, and glasses taken downstairs, the maggots and decaying food properly disposed of, the sheets washed, and the bed properly made and—what *is* that smell?"

"I'm sure it's nothing, Daddy. Okay, you go downstairs and I'll be there in ten minutes, and you can come up and—"

"It seems to be coming from the closet."

"The closet is very clean. You don't have to worry about—Daddy, don't open—"

"Good god in heaven!"

"It's okay. I'll clean it up."

"It's *far* from okay. You have a colony of rats living in your closet, feeding on garbage that is actual feet deep all over the floor. My god, I never realized roaches grew to that size! And a couple of feral cats are sleeping on the shelves. You have a whole native ecology in this one little room. I've never seen anything like this in my life."

"It does look a little messy, now that you mention it—"

"Messy? *Messy?* I'll bet there are garbage pits that are less messy than this. It looks more like a sewer than a clothes closet. You go right down to the garage, this instant, and get a shovel and start cleaning this out. I'll go to the store and buy a large box of reinforced trash bags and a fumigation kit."

"Can't we do this tomorrow? Please? I have to go to Carla's house right this minute, before she bursts from whatever news she has to tell me."

"Heavens no. I don't want the health inspectors to condemn our living space."

"Please? Pretty, pretty, pretty please?"

"I have an idea. Why don't you call Carla and tell her to come over? You can clean your room together. Maybe she knows a professional sanitation worker that she can bring with her."

Sigh. "Does it really mean that much to you?"

"Yes. It really does."

"You don't care that it's *my* room?"

"No. It's for your own good. I'm afraid this room is already breeding exotic jungle plagues and mutated vermin, and I simply won't stand for any more of it, not in my house."

"Okay, Daddy. Carla and I will tidy up the room."

"Good."

"Right when we get back from the mall."

Strict Rules

It's natural for daughters to want to invite their closest friends to spend the night, and the wise parent recognizes that it is easier to keep track of activities taking place in your own home than if your daughter is elsewhere.

However, the spend-the-night situation is not without complications. To avoid misunderstandings later on, you should probably make sure that the young guest is willing to live, albeit temporarily, under your (potentially more strict) household rules and regulations.

"What a great soccer game! You girls were terrific!"

"Thanks, Daddy."

"Six goals to four. I can hardly talk, my throat is so sore from shouting foul words at the referees."

"Daddy, this is Wanda. She scored one of our goals and broke the other team's midfielder's kneecap."

"Hi, Wanda. You played a nice game."

"Thanks."

"Daddy, can Wanda spend the night with us tonight?"

"I don't know. Wanda may not *want* to stay with us. Wanda, we're a little bit strict at our house. You might not be accustomed to having to live according to our rules."

"What do you mean?"

"Well, we have one really firm rule where Jasmine and her little friends can't send out for pizza after one o'clock in the morning on a school night. Not ever."

"Okay."

"Absolutely no exceptions."

"Daddy, I told her about our rules."

"Did you tell her that you girls absolutely have to be quiet while I'm doing your homework? Otherwise, there's no way I'll have it all finished in time. You'll just have to go upstairs to Jasmine's bedroom with your boyfriends until I'm done. And I expect you to be quiet up there."

"I think I can live with that, if Jasmine can."

"And we have very strict rules about drinking."

"I'm only twelve. I don't—"

"No drinking alcoholic beverages of any kind, whatsoever, outside the house. If you and Jasmine and your other preteen friends are going to get falling-down drunk and pass out on the couch, you're going to have to do it at home with whatever you can find in our liquor cabinet rather than some seedy bar or package store. No exceptions."

"Daddy—"

"It's all right if you want to back out because we're a little stricter than maybe you're used to. I understand."

"I think I might be able to handle it. For—for one night, anyway."

"All right, it's up to you. Just make sure you bring your homework. I don't want to hear any excuses about how I can't finish it because you forgot one of your books."

"Yes, sir."

Science Project

Most schools discourage parents from actively participating in their little girls' science projects. But the attentive father can contribute in many other ways to his daughter's success, helping her boost her self-esteem in the process.

"Daddy, could I talk to you for a minute?"

"Of course. I always have time for my little girl. What's this about?"

"I need you to look at my science project. We need to figure out how to move it to Mrs. Greenblot's classroom."

"I'm sure that won't be a problem. I'm pretty big and strong, and there's plenty of room in the—"

"This project has been *so* much trouble ever since I lost the eight breeding pairs of fleas in your bedroom. I had to improvise like crazy, just to get something done."

"Didn't you promise last year, after that incident with intestinal parasites, that we would talk about your science project *before* you started?"

"Yes, Daddy."

"So … what did you do this year? Please tell me it had nothing to do with the lunchroom."

"Of course not, silly. My first idea was to make a roadside bomb, using the plans from this Afghanistan website. They even send you the parts. So I figured, you know how everybody in school hates

Mr. Webster, the guidance counselor? I thought I could go into the parking lot—"

"That's exactly the kind of thing I wanted to talk to you about in advance. If you've done any property damage—"

"Cool it, Daddy. I realized all by myself that there would be other cars around, and some of them would belong to cool teachers, and it would be really hard to get the smoking remnants of Mr. Webster's car through the front door of the school."

"That's excellent judgment. So what, exactly, did you do with the dangerous explosives?"

"When I got the bomb parts, they also sent a bunch of really interesting chemicals that I thought maybe I could do something with. So I went on the Internet and found this site whose URL is made up of a bunch of skulls and crossbones, and they had even *more* interesting chemicals, and I was starting to feel a scientific curiosity about what I could do with them. It's a good thing I used your e-mail account and credit card, because right after I finished the transaction, people from the CIA started snooping around. But now there's no way they can trace those purchases to me."

"Maybe that would explain the truck with the big dish antenna parked across the street."

"Mom told me to take the chemicals downstairs to the basement, because some of them smelled bad and were giving off a greenish vapor."

"I'm still a little confused. What did you do for your science project?"

"I was just about to tell you. I mixed all the chemicals together, just to see what would happen."

"And?"

"They made a hole in the floor. It's really cool. You can shine a flashlight into it and the light just goes and goes and you still can't see the bottom. Sometimes you can hear the gurgling sound of lava, but it sounds like it's miles away."

"In our basement."

"Yes."

"Through the concrete floor."

"I think it went all the way through the crust and part of the mantle. See? It's turned into kind of a geology experiment, although that wasn't really the original plan."

"Okay, so I may have this straight now. You want me to transport a hole that is miles deep over to your middle school."

"That's right. I thought you could use a shovel or something."

"I have a better plan."

"What?"

"We'll get a lead weight at the hardware store and twenty or thirty skeins of kite string, and we'll carefully lower it over the side and measure the depth of the hole. We'll take pictures of it. How wide is the hole?"

"Maybe three feet across."

"We can lower a cell phone down in there and take pictures of geological layers and send them over to the local college for analysis."

"Oh, Daddy, you are *so* smart."

"And we can put a little fence around part of our basement to prevent any of our house guests from falling clear down to hell, and every night we can pray that there won't be a volcanic eruption from that gurgling noise you heard."

"You know how to fix everything."

"Except that other part of it."

"What?"

"The CIA truck across the street."

"Don't worry about that, Daddy. I took care of it already. They're going to get the surprise of their lives."

"What do you mean?"

"You remember those roadside bomb parts that I didn't use on Mr. Webster's car?"

"Yes. As a matter of fact, I do."

"I was going to tell you, in about forty seconds or so, it might be a good idea to duck under your desk."

Appropriate Attire

During the teenage years, your daughter's taste in clothing might undergo some visible changes as she strives for a more "mature" look that will at once communicate her independence and interest in the opposite gender. The parent's chief role during this complicated time is to serve as a wise counselor, gently indicating when, or if, the chosen attire seems inappropriately provocative.

"You're not going out dressed like that!"

"Daddy, do you always have to do that fake heart attack thing every time I go out the door?"

"Look at what you're wearing! What possible social event do you think it's appropriate to go out dressed like that?"

"I'm only going over to the football locker room for a beer-drinking contest while the players finish their showers. It's not a dress-up sort of thing."

"But you're not wearing any pants."

"You are *so* out of it. This is a G-string. Everybody's wearing them."

"Everybody? Name one person."

"Cindy Slutmeister."

"I thought Cindy left junior high to have her baby."

"Daddy! She's only seven months."

"Are there any *nonpregnant* people wearing G-strings in public?"

"Lots of them. Carol Ann's parents let her."

"Carol Ann's parents shot themselves last month. The suicide note said they'd take their chances that the afterlife would be easier than raising her."

"I don't understand what you want from me. If you'd just *try* to be reasonable."

"When I was your age, if I saw a girl wearing something like what you have on, I'd think she was loose and easy. Is that the kind of message you want to send?"

"Well, no."

"I didn't think so."

"How about if I spray-paint a little in back? Would that make you feel better?"

"Not as good as if you wore actual pants."

"Ohhhh. You're impossible. Why can't I wear what everybody else wears?"

"Because you're not everybody else. You're my wonderful, beautiful daughter."

"I'm a social outcast with repressive parents who want to drive me crazy about every little thing I do, who want to pick out the clothes I wear and decide what foods I should eat, and which drugs I should take and—"

"Drugs?"

"All right, Daddy, if you *insist* that I wear clothing, I'll go ahead and change into that cute microskirt that I just got on that turfeuse. com website."

"That's my good girl."

Divide and Conquer

The adolescent daughter might have occasional difficulty recognizing appropriate behavioral boundaries. If she believes that her parents are unnecessarily repressive, she might resort to a triangulation strategy, seeking permission independently from both parents, looking for inconsistencies in your judgment.

The key is to, first, let the child know that you are not fooled by this tactic, and then to present a clearly unified parental front.

"Daddy? Daddy?"

"Hmmmm?"

"Daddy, Jennifer's older brother has gotten permission from his probation officer to drive out to a biker's rally in the Grand Tetons. He says he'll be camping out on the open ground for about six days, unless the local police decide to make mass arrests—because of the drugs and all. Can I skip final exams and go with him?"

"Hmmm? What did your mother say?"

"I don't remember."

"What? Wait a minute, you don't remember whether you got permission from your mother?"

Sigh. "You caught me."

"I sure as heck did. Listen, you may think you can put these things over on us, asking your mom first and then asking me, and if you get conflicting answers, you just do whatever you want under the guise of having a 'yes' answer from a parent. But I'm on to you. I am a smart father, and you'll have to live a lot longer before you can outwit me."

"Yes, Daddy."

"So what do *you* think the answer is?"

"I have to go on this trip, even if I don't want to."

"That's my girl. Now get packing and leave me alone and don't ever try anything like that again."

"Wasn't that Jennifer's brother driving off with our daughter on a motorcycle?"

"I think so. Why?"

"He's thirty-four years old and has a prison record."

"How am I going to get anything done if you keep barging in here—"

"Did you tell her she could go?"

"Well, I asked her what you said first."

"I told her I'd fry in hell before she took a thousand-mile motorcycle ride in the dead of winter to sleep in the open with a bunch of violent, drug-abusing criminals before she's even fourteen years of age."

"Oh."

"And she came in here and got you to say it was all right."

"Well—"

"Why did I marry an idiot like you?"

"Because you loved me?"

"Don't push it."

"Maybe I should go chase them down on the freeway and have a talk with her."

"If you hurry, you can probably catch them before the divorce papers are finalized."

True Romance

From time to time, you may find yourself engaged with your daughter in a heartwarming discussion about teen romance. At such times, show a genuine interest in her chosen object of affection and the circumstances of her relationship with that special person. As she opens up to you about the first adolescent stirrings of young, innocent love, it will be as if a window into her private life has suddenly been thrown open. The two of you will share one of those rare moments of intimacy and mutual understanding.

"Who was that walking home with you today?"

"Bobby. He's on the football team."

"I thought you were going out with Elmer."

"Oh, Daddy, I thought you knew we broke up."

"Why? I kind of liked Elmer. He looked like the sort of boy that no girl would be interested in having physical relations with."

"He said he was getting the seven-day itch."

"But you only dated for, what? Three days? Or was it four?"

"Bobby's much more romantic. He always checks my cell phone to make sure I'm not texting any other boys. He was going to beat up a boy who looked at me in the hall, but the teachers broke it up before he could hurt anybody. Isn't that sweet?"

"He sounds like a thug. Has he ever been convicted of any violent crimes?"

"I told you he plays football. They don't let criminals on the football team unless they're really, really good."

"So ... what do you and Bobby do?"

"We haven't actually been on a date yet. Mostly we make out in the art room before school, because Mr. Michaels is such a cool art teacher that he doesn't care."

"Do you happen to have Mr. Michaels's phone number?"

"And we sit together at lunch, and he eats his lunch and mine and Cindy Ackerman's if she doesn't like what her mother made her, which is most of the time because she's anorexic, and then he makes Brian Switzer give him his lunch money so he can get three or four desserts. And we just talk whenever his mouth isn't full."

"That sounds very romantic. Are you looking for Mr. Michaels's phone number?"

"I'm texting him. I'm telling him that I really, really love him."

"As much as you loved Elmer?"

"Way more. Elmer was kind of dweeby."

"What is he saying?"

"He wants to know if I'll do his math homework. See? I told you he was romantic."

"How is *that* romantic?"

"It's his way of telling me that he admires my mind, not just my body. He and I, we can talk about anything. He'll tell me how he feels about the defensive line coach that day, and I'll tell him about how my girlfriend Sandy really likes this boy from another school, and it took us weeks, or at least days, to find somebody who knew a girl in that other school who could find out from one of his friends if he liked her too, only it turned out he likes somebody else, but she doesn't even know he likes her, and then we had to make this friend swear that she wouldn't tell him until Sandy has a chance to go to this party that we think he'll maybe be at on Saturday, and he'll tell me how much weight he can lift now and how much more that is than last week. We have really, really good conversations about stuff."

"You do have Mr. Michaels's phone number in there, don't you?"

"Sure, Daddy. Why do you want it?"

"If he's half as cool as you say he is, then I think it might be fun to talk to him."

"You can ask him about Bobby."

"I'll try to remember to do that."

Normal Behavior

There may come a time when your teenage daughter experiences mild feelings of embarrassment for reasons that you may find difficult to understand or relate to. At such times, the most important thing to remember is that she is experiencing a very real emotional pain. When this happens, your behavior should reflect a high level of sensitivity and discretion, particularly when you appear together in public places.

"I never did understand why you like it so much here at the mall. There's nothing but clothing stores for girls and hundreds of thousands of kids your age walking around dressed in a way that would embarrass a French prostitute. What do you *see* in this place?"

"Shhhh. Will you *please* act normal? You're embarrassing me."

"All I'm doing is walking along next to you."

"Try to do it in a normal way."

"That's another thing. I'm not totally clear on what you mean by 'normal.' I act exactly the way I do every other time, and pretty much the way I see every other adult acting, but you seem to be intensely, insanely embarrassed by it. I think maybe you have a different definition of 'normal' than I do."

"You are *so* embarrassing."

"Which means, I think, that I need to change my behavior."

"Isn't that what I've been telling you?"

"You know, in my normal behavior, I hardly ever try to sing opera at the top of my voice while I do a kind of belly dance while waving my arms around with my fingers pointed out. *Oh sola meeee-oooo. Oh sola youuuu-oooo.*"

"Daddy."

"Oh sola theyyyy-oooo."

"Daddy!!!"

"You don't have to shout at me. I can hear—"

"Shut up and put your hands down. Oh my god, don't *ever* dance like that again. People are *looking* at us."

"That was actually kind of fun. Who knew that acting normal could be—"

"That *wasn't* acting normal. It was the most embarrassing thing I've ever seen. It might have been the most embarrassing thing in the whole history of the world."

"I was just trying to act normal. Maybe if I took my shirt off—"

"Stop! What are you *doing!* Are you trying to *kill* me with embarrassment? Look. Just walk next to me. We'll go into a store and you'll just stand there, and you won't have an expression on your face, and you won't look at anybody except me when I try something on, and, instead of saying anything, you can just nod or shake your head a little bit to tell me whether you like it or not."

"And sing opera?"

"No! My god no."

"No dancing?"

"No."

"Just pretty much what I'm doing now."

"Right."

"Okay, now that I know what 'normal' is, we can get down to picking out your school clothes. How about this little number? It's perfect for you."

"That's a nun's habit."

"I think it would look cute on you."

"It's a little too conservative for me. How about this?"

"Those jeans are *torn!*"

"Daddy, they're made that way."

"But it's got a gaping hole the size of a bowling ball that shows off half of your butt. How about this instead?"

"Isn't that a burka, like the Arabian women wear?"

"Exactly! I think it would look beautiful on you."

"It looks like a large black tent. People wouldn't even know I'm in there. How about this?"

"Is that a dress or a large piece of cellophane? I can see right through it."

"Oh, Daddy. Everybody is wearing these."

"People are walking around *naked* in your school? I thought they had some kind of dress code."

Sigh. "What about this dress?"

"I think that's a top, not a dress."

"Look, see? It comes down almost to my hips."

"I think I'm going to sing another round of that opera thing."

"*No!* I mean, maybe we could look over here in this other part of the store. What about these jeans?"

"Do they absolutely have to have gashes and tears in them, as if you found them in the attic of an abandoned farmhouse?"

"Yes, Daddy."

Sigh. "Do you think you could pick out some tops that at least attempt to hide the physical details of your breasts?"

"Do you have to be so unreasonable?"

"I'm starting to feel like belly dancing, right here in the store."

"Let me see what I can find."

"I'll wait over here, trying not to make eye contact with anybody while you try them on."

"Don't talk to anybody either. Try to act normal."

"It won't be easy."

"*Tell* me about it."

Helping with Homework

Helping your daughter organize her schoolwork assignments is a classic example of how one shared activity can accomplish multiple goals. You communicate the importance of learning and meeting the expectations of her teachers, and you help her become more organized and efficient at handling complex tasks.

It is also an important bonding experience between father and daughter, as you share a part of her classroom experience in a supportive way.

"Daddy, can I watch a movie?"

"I told you, the movies are going to stay locked up with the cable box until you finish your homework."

"But I don't have any homework."

"Are you lying to me?"

"Daddy, I would never lie to you."

"Yes, you would. That's a lie right there."

"Okay, but I can do it all on the bus on the way to school. Please can I have the key to the steel vault?"

"First show me what you have to do. How about history?"

"Just a little research report."

"How little?"

"Only sixteen pages on the origins of totalitarianism. I already looked up one of the thirteen references I need. It's something about kings and queens."

"Uh-huh. What about French class?"

"I'm supposed to translate the first three volumes of something called *À la recherche du temps perdu* by somebody named Proust. But that class isn't until after lunch. I have plenty of time to get it done in homeroom."

"Math?"

"Twenty-five word problems."

"That's all?"

"And the test. But I plan to study while I'm changing out of my gym clothes second period."

"Don't you think you should do at least an hour of homework tonight before TV?"

"Will you help me? You're so smart."

"Well … I was wondering if you'd ever notice. Back when I went to school, I used to correct the teachers' questions on exams, and they were always pestering me to deliver guest lectures to the faculty—"

"You could help me with math. Here, I'll read the first problem, and you can work on it. If the moon is 380,000 kilometers from the earth and circles the earth at an orbital speed of 1.022 kilometers a second, how long would it take a rocket launched from Newark, New Jersey, when the moon is exactly overhead, to travel in a parabolic orbit to the farside surface—"

"Honey?"

"They give the mass of the rocket and the thrust ratio in this little table—"

"Darling?"

"Yes, Daddy?"

"Why don't you post that question online at the MIT alumni discussion forum, and I'll troll the Internet to see if any graduate students have a workable essay on totalitarianism that they could loan us."

"Okay, Daddy. Maybe I could post *all* the math problems."

"That's my girl. Take the initiative on your homework. Plus, I think we could download a perfectly workable English translation of Proust's masterpiece from Great Books Index. If we apply ourselves, we can have somebody else get all this done in about fifteen minutes."

"So what am I going to do in homeroom today?"

"Study for the math test, or download an app to your phone that will do the test for you."

"Boy, you really *are* smart."

"Well, I don't like to toot my own horn, but back when I was in the first grade, college professors would—"

"Daddy?"

"—ask my advice about deep philosophical—"

"Daddy!"

"What."

"If you want, you can go get the key to the movies while I upload these questions."

"Right."

The Talk

Your instincts will tell you when it's time to have "that conversation" with your teenage daughter. Remember to keep the discussion factual and on point, while trying to avoid judgmental or prejudicial comments that might adversely affect her ability to, in the fullness of time, physically bond with that special someone.

"Honey?"

"Yes, Daddy?"

"Now that you've finally made it, alive, past your fifteenth birthday, I think we need to have The Talk."

"What talk is that, Daddy?"

"Well, it's hard to know where to begin. Do you remember when you asked about where babies came from, and we had that long talk about the stork? Well, that wasn't exactly the total truth—"

"Oh, I know *that*."

"You do?"

"It's all explained on the rap albums, and they even have it illustrated in some of their videos. You see, the gangsta looks across the club and sees this hot bitch, and pretty soon they're out in the alley, and he rips the skimpy little dress off of her even though she's not wearing underwear—"

"Okay. *Okay!* I mean, actually, the most important part of The Talk was not the *mechanics* of it, but mostly to make sure you understood that all guys are basically horrible scum."

"What do you mean?"

"I mean, they look at you, and all they see are … certain body parts, and they want … you know … your body, and it's really disgusting."

"You mean, like, Adonis Cooper is looking at me that way in the hallway?"

"Scum. Horrible scum."

"Do you think that's also true about Gravis Marks, who just signed that modeling contract?"

"Scum. They're all scum."

"I never imagined that hot guys like that were interested in my body in that way."

"Well, now you know."

"You're sure of this?"

"All they want to do is sleep with you. But they won't be sleeping—believe me."

"Oh my god, this is *so* exciting. Hold on while I text my friend Emily—no, maybe not. Maybe I shouldn't share this with *anybody* until I can put it to good use."

"What do you mean?"

"Oh, Daddy, thank you so much." *Kiss.* "You've made me *so* happy."

"So you'll remember what I said, right?"

"I won't forget a word of it."

"Promise?"

"Pinkie swear and hope to die. Oh my god, I can hardly wait to go to school tomorrow."

Greeting the Boyfriend

Few parents can ever hope to fully master the complex ritual of meeting and greeting a daughter's date. It's natural to feel protective toward your little girl, while at the same time recognizing that she's capable of making adult decisions and choices, and that her taste in members of the opposite gender may not be perfectly in sync with yours.

This is a moment that calls for equal parts tact and discretion, overlaid with a certain subtle firmness of tone that helps establish the parental boundaries you intend to set on the dating experience. Even though she may not express this clearly, your daughter will secretly appreciate this visible evidence that you love and care about her well-being and safety.

Doorbell rings.

"Will you get the door, dear? It's probably our little girl's date. He's early, and she's still upstairs getting ready."

"Sure. Okay."

"And try to be more positive with this one. Don't get your shotgun out."

"All right. All right."

"Hello. I'm Jasmine's dad. Those are ... nice tattoos."

"Thanks."

"Come in. Jasmine's not ready. You and I can sit on the couch and get to know each other."

"Jasmine told me I didn't have to do that."

"She what?"

"She said you had really old-fashioned ideas about teenage sex and birth control and mind-altering drugs, and to the extent that it was possible, I should pay no attention to you."

"Hold on right there while I get my shotgun."

"Hi, Brewski! You're early! How come you don't have a shirt on?"

"Hey, Jasmine, your dad and I were just talking, and I was just about to tell him that I'm taking you to a fancy restaurant where they actually have people that bring the food to your table and stuff."

"I'm in a dress and you're wearing *that*? You look like you just climbed out of a Dumpster! Daddy, will you put that gun away?"

"I thought maybe if I threatened him with death, he'd go away, or at least take a shower."

Sigh. "Okay. Go ahead."

"Look, you, can you see my eye in the sight of this shotgun? If you look very carefully down the borehole, you can see how serious I am. You go home right now, take a shower, put on a tuxedo, get those tattoos cleaned off of you, shave the rest of your head, get a job as a midlevel executive at a Fortune 500 company, and then come back and show my little girl a good time in a way that doesn't involve either of you touching each other until and unless you get married in a house of worship of our choosing. Do you hear me?"

"Yes, sir. Is that thing really loaded?"

"It has a nuclear missile in each barrel. They're very expensive, but definitely worth it for situations like this."

"I'll be back in fifteen minutes. Can you wait that long?"

"I'll just go upstairs and put on some more makeup—and wax myself"—*giggle*—"you know where."

Giggle. "I do. Bye, sir."

"Good-bye."

The New Sound

It is a rite of passage for every emerging adolescent to bond with the music of her generation. In many cases, the parent may have difficulty relating to her choices, just as your parents might have been reluctant to accept your own taste in music when you were growing up.

Try not to be judgmental, and learn to appreciate the new sound that fuels the tribal rhythms of your daughter's peers.

"Goodness gracious, I thought somebody was strangling chickens up here. Does your MP3 player have to be turned up so loud?"

"Daddy, if I put my earbuds in, Carla wouldn't be able to listen too."

"I can't hear you."

"I said that Carla likes to listen to the music."

"There. That's more of an acceptable volume. At least the windows downstairs aren't rattling and the dog can come out from under the couch. What *is* that group, anyway?"

"The Prison Escapees. They are *so* cool. Except now I can hardly hear what they're going to do to the Pope."

"Don't the instruments sound to you like random noise?"

"Those are automatic weapons and tire irons beating against skulls."

"Oh. Back in my day, they used guitars and drums and—"

"That was a long time ago, Daddy."

"Now what are they singing about?"

"Animal sacrifices."

"Good lord—"

"Should we change albums? Let's see … I have the Violent Misfits, or the Reign of Horror album, or we could listen to Princes of Evil …"

"If you want, I could download some really groovy tunes onto your MP3."

"Like what?"

"Oh, the choices are endless. How about the Beatles? *Obladee, Obladaa, life goes on, la! La, la, la, la, la, la, goes on …*"

"Ew. Is that what your dad listened to when he was young?"

"I think he must have been kind of a dweeb. Here, Daddy. We'll play Assured Destruction. It's kind of tame."

"Or maybe The Guess Who. *Clap for the Wolfman.* " *Clap, clap.* "*He gonna rate your record high … You're gonna dig him til the day you die …* Wait a minute. Did they just sing something about blowing up the Grand Canyon?"

"It's mostly about sex and hating girls even though they need hot bitches to satisfy their angry animal desires."

"Couldn't you listen to something more … upbeat?"

"This is our music. It's the music that is shaping our generation."

"So you're going to be a generation of destructive misfits?"

"Isn't that a little judgmental?"

"Listen. Now they're singing a tribute to anthrax."

"Daddy, did your parents hate the music you listened to?"

"Well, sometimes, yes. But it was pretty tame compared to this."

"Didn't you think *their* music was kind of lame?"

"It *was* lame."

"Did you let them tell you what to listen to?"

"Absolutely not. I demanded my right to listen to the Archies and the 1910 Fruitgum Company, no matter what they said."

"And what did they do?"

"They took away my radio."

"Wow! And how did that make you feel?"

"I felt like I was cut off from the tribal drums of my generation.

I felt lost and alone, like I didn't have an identity. I would sit on my bed and say 'boogey woogey' to myself over and over again."

"So can you see where I'm going with this?"

"No."

"How about if we compromise?"

"That's the spirit. I'll go and download—"

"You can play your own MP3 player with the earbuds in, and you can play anything you want."

"Anything at all?"

"The Beatles, the fruit thing, guess what, whatever you like."

"Are you sure? Some of those songs are about controversial things like … like kissing someone even if you aren't married, and stopping wars and things."

"It's your generation's music. You should be able to tune into the heartbeat of your peers whenever you want to."

"That's … very open-minded of you. Nobody has actually ever said that to me before. My dad still says my music is nothing but a bunch of bums who can't carry a tune."

"And how did *that* make you feel?"

"I still get annoyed when he says it. And you should hear what *he* listens to."

"Your music is all right for you, just like his music was all right for him. Just like ours is all right for us."

"And we're all okay, right?"

"And since the earbuds are delivering your music right into your ears, you won't even hear us playing 'Tear Down Civilization, Part Seven.'"

"I do like to play 'Yummy Yummy Yummy' at high volume. I like to really crank up the bass—"

"I'm glad we had this talk, Daddy."

"Me too. I feel … empowered somehow. If you ever need any advice on groovy kinds of things to listen to, you just let me know."

"We'll think about it."

"That's my girl."

Improving Your Wardrobe

A s your daughter moves into her midteenage years, it is perfectly normal for her to notice that you don't totally conform to her adolescent concept of coolness. She may even begin offering suggestions on appropriate attire.

The wise and sensitive parent should listen attentively and perhaps even accept some of her helpful suggestions concerning your wardrobe.

"Daddy, why do you wear that sweatshirt all the time?"

"I like it. It's comfortable."

"Didn't anybody ever tell you that you look kind of nerdy in it?"

"No."

"Well, they should have."

"I think when you look nerdy *all the time*, people don't really get into the particulars about which article of clothing you're wearing. It's like, you never hear anybody say, 'Look at this! There's air all around me today!' Or 'Wow, did you notice that there's ground under our feet today?' They don't really feel the need to comment on those things, and they don't tell me I look nerdy either."

"Maybe if you wore different clothing—"

"Wait a minute … didn't *you* buy me this sweatshirt?"

"Daddy, I was five years old at the time. It was sweet of you to wear it all these years, but maybe now you can switch to something else."

"How about this?"

"You don't see people wearing long-sleeved tie-dyed shirts very often anymore."

"Okay, well, there's my Nehru jacket, and these leather pants—"

"Maybe it would save time if I just went through your closet and threw out anything that looks, you know, like you have no sense of fashion or style or even know what century you're living in."

"Would there be anything left in there?"

"Maybe not."

"Is it possible that some people were never intended to be cool?"

"Daddy, what are you saying?"

"I mean, look at *you*. You have a terrific sense of where to pierce parts of your body and exactly where to apply a tattoo and what it should look like. Your clothes are torn in all the right places, and when you hold them together with safety pins, the safety pins and the way they're arranged looks way stylish."

"Yeah. So?"

"You have style and fashion genes that I just don't have. If I got a tattoo, it would probably be nothing but words, like 'Respect Old People.' If my clothes had holes in them, I wouldn't know if they were *fashionable* holes or just signs that the fabric was wearing out. The best thing you and your fashion sense could do is feel sorry for me and move on to somebody more promising."

"I can't just leave you like this. At least take off that ridiculous sweatshirt with the picture of Horton the Elephant on it."

"And change into—what?"

"Let me get a pair of scissors and some safety pins, and I'll take a look around your closet. I'll be back in a couple of hours."

"Don't make me look *too* cool."

"If I were you, I wouldn't worry too much about that."

The Dreaded Driver's Test

It may be hard for a parent to recall the degree of anxiety that surrounded your first driver's test, which would either grant freedom and mobility and adult responsibility, or deny it. Now, as your daughter climbs into the car, it may become a time of anxiety all over again, for very different reasons. Your daughter is taking a major step closer to full independence and at the same time participating, at a very young age, in one of the most dangerous activities condoned by our society.

Try to remember that your daughter will be depending on your full support throughout the testing process and will look for your approval regardless of the outcome.

"Daddy, is the line *always* like this at the driver's license place?"

"Sometimes it's worse. I remember once when I was here to get my license renewed, I started a conversation with the person next to me and then looked over and realized I was talking to a skeleton with cobwebs all over it."

"Really?"

"Look, already you're … what—103rd in line? And we've only been waiting here for four hours. It gives you more time to study that little booklet."

"I'm *so* nervous. What if I don't pass the driving test?"

"Then you'll have to wait another month to take it over again, and for that month, the world will be a much safer place."

"Maybe we should go back outside and practice parallel parking. I think I might be able to do it this time without hitting other cars."

"Look. Now you're 102nd in line."

"The testing person is so old. And he looks really grumpy. What if he doesn't like me?"

"Trust me. He doesn't care about you. All he wants to do is survive one more day at this job. Now study your booklet."

"Okay, Daddy."

"I'll be right back."

"Okay, darling, you're next."

"I'm what? How can that be?"

"I paid everybody in front of you twenty bucks to come back tomorrow."

"Wow! I'm excited. I hope he likes me."

"You go ahead and show him your learner's permit. I'll wait here."

"Well, that didn't take long. How did it go?"

"Ohmigod, he was *so* mean. It was horrible."

"What do you mean, horrible? Didn't you pass?"

"No. He failed me."

"What did you do?"

"Nothing. He just hated me."

"Let me see the test results. Wait a minute; this isn't a test report. It's a criminal citation."

"I told you he was mean to me."

"I'm having trouble reading the writing. Does that say something about scattering pedestrians under your wheels like chickens? Wait … you collided with an *ambulance*? And the … what's this? Where's the car? I don't see it anywhere in the parking lot—"

"It's laying facedown in a little stream in the woods, because when I backed up to do the parallel parking thing—oh, Daddy, this is the most horrible day of my life. Could you, maybe, go back in and talk to him? He was *so* mean to me."

"Come on. Let's borrow a car and go home."

Party Central

It is almost a rite of passage for the maturing adolescent to take control of the home while her parents travel out of town. When you return, casually but thoroughly inspect the house for hidden clues that it might have been used for inappropriate activities.

"Did you guys have a party here while we were out of town?"

"No, Daddy. Of course not."

"You're sure."

"Why do you ask?"

"Parts of the house have severe fire damage and one whole interior wall is missing. It looks like somebody took a sledgehammer to it."

"Oh, *that*."

"And the living room is flooded with a liquid that appears to be beer. It's at least three inches deep in some of the larger puddles near that keg. Also, I'm pretty sure we didn't have a three-quarters–empty beer keg in the living room when we left."

"Daddy, don't you trust me?"

"You *did* have some friends over. Didn't you?"

"Carla and Emily came over to watch TV."

"That's it?"

"They brought their boyfriends. And their boyfriends had a few friends."

"How many, exactly?"

"I lost count after three hundred, but the police said there were more."

"The *police*?"

"They were mostly just confiscating the drugs. They actually said we were pretty well-behaved once the fire department had left. Oh, I almost forgot. They said you should call them. Something about not having a liquor license and they wanted to speak to you about the county noise ordinances. They made the marching band go home, so Carla's boyfriend figured out how to rewire the sound system so it wouldn't burn out if we added a few thousand amps—"

"Didn't I tell you, when we left, that there would be *no parties* in this house while we were gone?"

"Yes, Daddy."

"Didn't I specifically say something about not burning the house down?"

"Yes, Daddy. But the structural damage—"

"No buts. I thought I was very clear."

"You were. I'm sorry."

"Not as sorry as you're going to be. I'm very disappointed in you. From now on, you're going to have your wings clipped."

"But, Daddy—"

"I mean it. From now on, you're totally grounded. No dates past two o'clock in the morning on school nights. I'm taking away your fake ID card for … for a *week*. If you want to drink with your friends, you'll have to do it in what's left of our basement."

"Yes, Daddy. Don't you think that's a little harsh?"

"I'm not even finished yet. From now on, you have to tell us before you go out of town on the weekends. No more phone calls asking for plane fare back from the Caribbean. And don't start crying either. That's not going to change my mind."

"Yes, Daddy."

"Now go up to the unburned half of your room and get busy on your homework."

"Daddy?"

"What now?"

"I'm really, really sorry. I really, really am."

"You ought to be."

"Now that you know how sorry I am, can I have my fake ID back?"

The College Interview

For girls who want to go on to higher education, choosing a college can be an exciting but stressful experience. The parent's role is to help the daughter see the bigger picture, to match educational opportunities to her preferred field of study, taking into consideration issues like proximity to home and family, the size and affordability of the school, and the potential distractions that could derail her college career before it gets started.

"Honey, this is Mr. Doxflagger. He's a college admissions officer here who was gracious enough to give us this appointment."

"I'm glad to meet you. Your father says you have an interest in attending our university?"

"He thinks I need to go to college in order to amount to something. This is all his stupid idea."

"Interesting. I can see that you'll make an A in candor."

"She doesn't really mean that. She's eager to expand her educational horizons."

"I did too mean it. I mean, how is this not just a four-year waste of time and a whole lot more homework?"

"Well, I can say from my professional observation that the students who come here often start out skeptical about the benefits of a university education. But over the course of four years—or really five, since nobody actually graduates in four years anymore—those same students blossom and begin to realize that it's a lot easier and cozier to have their parents pay the bills rather than have to go out and face the harsh job market and work forty-hour weeks instead of sleeping through three classes a day. Why, we have students who basically come here and never leave. They get an undergraduate degree and then take their time about getting a master's degree, before leisurely pursuing higher designations in a process that can extend out to decades."

"Do they have to do homework all that time?"

"It depends entirely on your field of study. We have an excellent bird-watching curriculum that is very popular with the members of our football team, and many of our chronic slackers and misfits find their way to the journalism department. But even if you decide to pursue a degree with actual future career prospects, it can't possibly be that challenging. Take a look around and you'll see a lot of students lounging around the lawns or the recreational building all afternoon, trying to attract the attention of the opposite gender. And the dance halls in town are always packed to capacity."

"Really?"

"I don't think I'm boasting when I point out that our institution has held up extremely well in the Top Party School rankings. In fact, we were eliminated from consideration this year because the editors concluded that it wouldn't be fair to include us in an amateur contest when our students appear to be party professionals."

"Tell me more about the dance halls. Do they let underage students drink?"

"I think I should interrupt here. The truth is, my daughter is extremely talented at dissemination and manipulation. I thought maybe a legal career would suit her best."

"Yes, of course. We have many different prelaw curricula, and of course the law school itself has produced some of the finest legal minds in the country, with a particular emphasis on criminal defense of scumbags and Wall Street executives."

"That sounds hard."

"A large part of what we call 'developing essential skills' is learning to negotiate grades with your professors after you've behaved scandalously. We've found that it's excellent real-world training for the type of clients our graduates tend to represent."

"Do they let boys in the dorms after midnight?"

"Yes, I think that's an excellent question my daughter is asking. I noticed that there aren't any large fences around the female dormitories, or vicious dogs patrolling the perimeter."

"We take all precautions to make sure that our coed students are not troubled by steaming-hot muscular members of our various athletic teams no matter how excited these semiprofessional athletes might become by the 'new blood' on campus."

"You know, Daddy, this college life doesn't sound so terrible after all. What do I have to do to apply?"

"Well, I have your transcript right here in the files, including the financial aid form, which really tells me all I need to know about your father's ability to pay your tuition regardless of whether you ever set foot inside a classroom. I see that you had a few irregularities in high school ... oh my."

"What?"

"I find myself wondering, given some of the spotty places on this transcript, including this affidavit from a teacher that your daughter assaulted—with a switchblade? And this lengthy discussion of explosives ... most irregular ..."

"Please, Daddy, can I go here?"

"What are you wondering, exactly?"

"Well, to be perfectly frank, some of these applications are really judgment calls. If your daughter weighed more than three hundred pounds of solid muscle and had played defensive end on her high school football team, I would have no problem overlooking criminal activities. As it is—"

"Please, Daddy?"

"I have three hundred dollars in my pocket. That's all I brought with me. We were going to use it for meals and gas money."

"I think that will be sufficient for a case like this. As it happens, given the nature of the student, I can also expect a kickback from the dance club for referring promising young wild party animals. If I give your daughter these two complimentary admission tickets and a coupon for two free underage drinks—"

"Thank you. That's very thoughtful. Isn't he nice, Daddy?"

"Well, if there's nothing more—"

"So she's accepted?"

"Welcome to college, young lady."

Commencement Exercises

For many families, a proud and singular moment comes at high school graduation, when your little girl formally completes what might be considered basic training for life. This accomplishment is shared with the friends and fellow travelers with whom your daughter has experienced so many happy times.

Your role during the ceremony is simply to allow feelings of pride to merge with similar feelings among the other parents in the ceremony's audience.

"I can't believe it. They're going to let you graduate after all."

"Daddy, do you always have to be so sentimental and melodramatic?"

"I'm very proud of you. I wasn't sure you would survive to this age, much less navigate through the school system."

"How do I look in this cap and gown?"

"Just like everybody else. Only much prettier."

"You're so sweet. I can hardly wait to give the valediction address thing."

"The what?"

"It's the speech that—"

"I know what it *is*. But you weren't even in the top half of your graduating class, thanks to that awful cheating scandal in your junior year. So how is it that—"

"Myron Winklebraster is a total wimp. I told him that if he didn't let me give the speech instead, I'd tell everybody that I tried to have sex with him, but he was impotent. He started crying, right there in the boy's locker room."

"But didn't the principal—"

"It's going to be a surprise. Nobody knows about it except Myron and me."

"Did you actually write a speech?"

"I memorized it. It wasn't hard."

"I see. Well, they're gathering everybody together. You'd better get in line."

"I say, is that your daughter in the graduation line?"

"As a matter of fact, it is."

"Darn!"

"I beg your pardon?"

"A few of us parents had a betting pool that she wouldn't make it out of high school. I guess I can kiss that fifty bucks good-bye."

"As a matter of fact, she's to give the valedictory address."

"What? You're kidding, right? Wasn't she in that cheating—"

"It was all a misunderstanding. Anyway, here she is now."

"Fellow students, graduates, parents, grandparents, coaches, administrators, faculty, and anybody else who might have wandered in here by mistake, here we are at the graduation ceremony. Look at us! I'll bet a lot of you teachers are really happy to see some of us go, and I know I speak for a lot of the students when I say that we won't be weeping any tears over not having to put up with any of your rear ends again."

"Wow! She gets right to the point. What are you doing under the chair?"

"Is it over yet? Please tell me it's over."

"I know we will all carry forward memories of, like, when Miss Senestra basically fell asleep when she was giving us a physics lecture, and how we all got away with cheating on the Algebra II final exam, or that fire in the chemistry laboratory that resulted in the school's third floor being declared a toxic waste site for three weeks by the Environmental Protection Agency. I doubt Jayme Mathers will ever in his life forget being held upside down over the toilet every couple of days by the wrestling team. I, myself, will carry forth happy memories of that incredible food fight the one time they were dumb enough to serve baked potatoes in the lunchroom, or that really big fistfight after we lost the football game to Valhalla High School. And, hey, you remember when they decided to do drag races in the school parking lot while school was just letting out, and it turned into this amazing demolition derby thing, and later we found out that the whole incident was written up as a case study in the professional publication of auto insurance underwriters?"

"I didn't know that."

"She borrowed our car to drive to school that day. There's a picture of some charred pieces of it on page forty-nine of that issue. I still have the article if you ever want to see it."

"Today, we look forward to a new stage of our lives, without a lot of stupid rules and the kind of regimentation that you normally only find in federal prisons, and teachers who are, like, totally obsessed with what an 'adverb' is or how to do something or other with the stupid 'cosine,' which I promise you I will never again have to even think about because it is so totally unrelated to anything in the real world. We go forth with our diploma packed away in some closet somewhere, and we'll carry with us a lot of resentment and anger, not just at the school administration for all the punishments we received for basically nothing except being kids our age, but also at our fellow students, who were so mean to us in what was basically a social environment where we were all routinely doing emotional damage to each other when we weren't having sex. Our future is before us, including a lot of wild parties this very evening, which reminds me that everybody is invited over to Joey Migrand's house because his parents are out of town and Caroline has a fake ID and managed to score a lot of beer and cheap wine, so we can celebrate this graduation thing in style."

"She's done. Please let her be done."

"On this very special occasion, let us all give our heartfelt thanks to god that the whole damn awful four-year ordeal—or, in the case of some students like Vinnie DeVito, six or seven—is finally over and we can move on with our lives, which is something most of us have been looking forward to basically since about the eighth grade. We leave behind us a bunch of underclasspeople who I know would give anything to be up here with us now because they've been telling us that for weeks, and some of them are just dying of envy, just like I was last year and the year before at about this time.

"But you know what? *You're all invited to the party at Joey's house too!* Even if you have another screwed-up year or two of putting up with these loser teachers of ours, you can at least watch us and see what it's like to be finally free and look forward to your own graduation, or just get so drunk and happy that it's finally summer that you won't really care what you have to look forward to. We can forget everything we learned over four long years in one wild night! Let's all give the cheer: *Party! Party! Party! Party! Party! Party!*"

"You can get up now. She seems to be finished."

"How was it? It's hard to hear exactly when you're curled up in a fetal position."

"The principal looks a trifle angry, but I think the audience kind of liked it. It reminds me of how I felt when we graduated."

"Really?"

"In fact, it started me to wondering."

"About what?"

"Do you think they'll let parents in that party at Joey what's-his-name's house?"

Campus News

One of the toughest aspects of parenting a college student is monitoring grades from afar and providing encouragement or long-distance discipline depending on your daughter's academic performance.

"Hi, Daddy. Look, before you get all upset and start worrying about why I'm calling you in the middle of the night, I just want you to know that the doctors say there's at least a 20 percent chance that I'll recover the use of my legs."

"What? Oh my god—"

"They also said they're working wonders with prosthetic devices these days, in case the limb reattachment doesn't go so well."

"Wait—I have to sit down."

"Are you okay, Daddy?"

"Can you just—just tell me what happened?"

"I guess it started when the police came and found all these drugs under Rachel's bed when they raided our dorm. None of them were mine, but since I'm her roommate, they issued a felony warrant for my arrest. But since I wasn't there at the time—"

"Wait. *Wait!* Hold on a minute. You said a warrant—"

"For my arrest. But as I said, I was out at the time, so Rachel called me from the station and said they were being really mean to her, so she agreed to plea-bargain and tell them that the drugs were all mine, and they've given her something called 'immunity,' whatever that is, and she says it feels great and could I please come down to the station?"

Gulp. Gasp. "Okay—"

"So of course being a law abiding citizen, I immediately got in the car to drive down there, but I had been at the bar for a few hours, and I'd been drinking maybe a little too much, so I maybe wasn't driving as carefully as I should have been when I sort of like ran into the side of the police station, but I really don't believe my blood alcohol level was high enough to kill a moose, as that awful district attorney told the grand jury—"

"There's a *grand jury* involved? Oh no—"

"That's what Rachel said, because I was in the hospital while she was testifying, where I think I told you they spent eight hours replenishing my blood supply and trying to stitch my legs back on, which is kind of expensive, so I was wondering if—"

"Have you got a lawyer? How do you feel? Can I talk to a doctor? Are you—"

"Calm down, Daddy. It sounds like you're hyperventilating. Maybe you should call Rachel. She said there are some drugs that the SWAT team didn't find, and she might be able to send some to you as a favor for me taking the rap."

"I just want to know you're okay. *Please* tell me you're okay, and then we'll start trying to dig you out of this—this—this unbelievable mess …"

"Daddy, are you crying?"

"Oh my god, what can I do—"

"You *are* crying. That's so sweet."

"I'll—I'll mortgage the house and then liquidate my retirement plan at work, and maybe we can get the hospital to extend the medical payments over thirty years so I can use some of that money to hire a good criminal attorney—"

"You'd do that for me?"

"Of course I would. Oh, oh, god in heaven—"

"Would it make you feel better if I told you that my legs are really totally okay?"

"What do you mean?"

"They weren't really injured."

"Thank god! You mean, they didn't get severed or even bruised or anything in the accident?"

"It wasn't really an accident even."

"Thank goodness! Yes, I *do* feel better. Now we can focus on the criminal investigation and your DUI—"

"Actually, there wasn't a DUI. I decided not to drive when I left the bar."

"Really? Seriously? That was a *terrific* decision. I'm so proud of you!"

"Thanks, Daddy. And the drug thing and federal warrant? I might have exaggerated that too. When I first got here, I had this roommate named Rachel who had some interesting drug habits, but after the first two weeks, I switched rooms with a girl named Gisele, and Gisele and Rachel got busted last week."

"No drug charges? I can hardly believe it! What great judgment to move out like you did! Honey, I—I can't really talk right now. I feel so much better about things. I need some air. I think maybe my heartbeat is irregular, the way I can suddenly feel the blood moving into and out of my fingers and toes. What does it mean when you can actually hear your heartbeat?"

"Really, the only thing that went wrong all week is I got a D on my chemistry test, which will probably give me a D for the course, and I'll probably have to take chemistry all over again."

"But you have your legs! And there isn't a pending criminal investigation!"

"I'm still a little bummed. And I thought maybe you'd be angry with me."

"Honey, instead of dwelling on this little grade setback, you should be counting your blessings. Look at the big picture! I can't tell you how good I feel about how you're doing at college."

"You're not mad?"

"I'm happy! How could I be mad when I'm so ecstatic that my little girl is all right?"

"I love you, Daddy."

"Do you need any money? I have money, right here in my pocket, where I can also feel my heartbeat, for some reason ..."

"You know, now that you mention it ..."

Looking Back, Looking Ahead

Your daughter's maturation process and your parenting have a logical ending, which all too few parents are able to recognize: the time when it is no longer appropriate for you to control her behavior. At this point, she has graduated from the parenting process and achieved full adulthood.

Of course, this doesn't end your relationship; it only changes it. You find yourself offering the benefit of your wisdom and experience, and you will be socializing with your daughter as an equal rather than an authority figure.

This is often an invisible threshold, but you can make it more relevant by celebrating and acknowledging her crossing, reminiscing and sharing happy memories about the now-completed process of raising her to adulthood.

"Look at all these people! You didn't tell me what a big deal this is."

"Your mom said you were between relationships right now, so I thought maybe you'd enjoy getting out of the house. And this is one of my favorite events of the year. They invite everybody—diplomats, college students, corporate executives, even the homeless are welcome to join in. They call it the Big Dance, and this year it's a square-dance theme."

"CEOs and firemen bold, on the floor, there's hands to hold ..."

"See that man over there? I think I've seen him in a magazine before. Bill something."

"Gates. I told you they get interesting people. That woman he's swinging around is the vice chairman of Hewlett Packard."

"Oh, my god, I think that's Donald Trump. But … what's that *thing?*"

"It's his latest wife. I read somewhere that he ordered her out of a Victoria's Secret catalog."

"Oh, Daddy. I was talking about the thing on his head."

"Oh. That appears to be either a piece cut out of a llama rug or a very inexpensive hairpiece."

"Why do they have everybody square-dancing?"

"I have no idea. It's different every year."

"Did Mom really say I needed a date?"

"Yes."

"Now hoboes dance with heads of state, swing them round, don't be late …"

"Did you see that funny Asian man trying to keep both his feet moving in the same direction?"

"He's the Chinese minister of defense."

"He's not a very good dancer."

"I suspect he's way more adept at deploying armored tank divisions and ballistic missiles."

"Now city clerks and teachers dance, kick your feet, make romance …"

"Your mom said you were getting a little scared about the future."

"Not scared, exactly. I keep thinking about all the things I want to do, all the things I want to be, and every time I make a plan, the very first thing that happens, sometimes the very next day, is that I'm back at square one, even before I'd had a chance to get to square two."

"You're actually making plans?"

"I see where you are today, and maybe it's not really where I want to go, but you've gotten so far from square one and two, and there are times when I think, when I get old like him, I'll have done a whole lot more. And other times I wonder if I'll ever even get started. It's really confusing."

"Tell me you didn't use the word 'old' in that last sentence."

"Architects, carpenters, come on down, now's the time to swing around ..."

"I thought I knew what I'd be by now."

"You are."

"What do you mean?"

"I mean, you're always who you are—nothing more or less. And you are always evolving, changing, growing, becoming; there is no destination, just a journey."

"At last we come to the real divide, fathers, daughters, dance with pride ..."

"That's us."

"Yes."

"Oh my god, that was exhausting. It was like pairing up with everybody for a second or two. I was watching you; you could actually dance."

"Not real dancing. But this square dancing is more like controlled walking with a skip to it."

"Now what?"

"They start over with different pairings. You'll be dancing with the Russian ambassador in a few minutes. Don't let him grope you."

"Do you understand anything at all about what I'm saying? Or am I the only person who ever felt this way?"

"What I really think is that despite my best efforts, despite all my hard work and diligent attention to responsible parenthood, somehow you still managed to turn out all right in the end."

"Sometimes it wasn't easy, ignoring your advice or sneaking around behind your back."

"Nobody ever said being parented is a walk in the park."

"City clerks and architects, join the dance and do your best ..."

"But you're really proud of me? You like the way I turned out in spite of everything?"

"I am. I do. I mean that sincerely."

"And this is what you hoped I would become?"

"Well, you haven't been elected to the White House, and I don't think you've been awarded the Nobel Peace Prize yet, and I was hoping to retire on the money you made when you took your immensely profitable start-up company public—"

"Those aren't totally realistic expectations."

"—but you're a good person with a good head on your shoulders who cares about others and takes care of yourself, and if everybody fit that description, this world would be a much better place. And the funny thing is that I never really doubted that you would someday get to this place you are now, in spite of the occasional disagreements about minor things like premarital sex and hygiene."

"There were times in my life when, if you approved of me or what I was doing, I got scared that I was conforming too much to what you expected, and I'd work really hard to change whatever you approved of. But now I'm only mildly concerned."

"That's my girl. You're growing up."

"CEOs and hoboes dance, here's your chance to find romance ..."

"Promise me one thing."

"What."

"Someday I'll be old—that is, I'll be your age—and my kids will be grown, and I'll have all these memories of them growing up like you have of me, only I'll have done a way better job, because I know all the tricks that I played when I was a kid, and I won't be nearly as uptight or gullible as you were."

"I can't tell you how flattering that is. So what am I promising, exactly?"

"Promise me that if you're still around, you'll remind me to take them to this dance and to tell them what you told me today. I want them to know what you've allowed me to know: that in spite of all the horrible pain they caused, and all the work and effort I put into them for all those years, that it was all worth it."

"Well ..."

"It *was* worth it, wasn't it?"

"I don't want to lie ..."

"Daddy."

"Firemen swing with carpenters, hurry down, the floor is yours."

"Yes."

"Yes what?"

"Yes, it was worth it. Yes, somehow, I got more out of it than I put into it, and I put in my heart and soul and probably shortened my life span by a decade or two and certainly made my hair gray twenty years before it would otherwise have happened on its own, and don't get me started on all the football games I missed—and, where was I going with this again?"

"Daddy."

"The bottom line is that over all those years, you enriched my life in ways I never imagined possible. And I'll remind you to tell that to your own kids, because it will be true, and also because hearing those words will just blow them away."

"Why will it blow them away?"

"Because I can see already that you're going to be a crabby, uptight mom who will freak out over little things like coming home and finding major structural damage to the house that you unwisely left in the hands of your teenage kids, and before you tell them this, they'll think they were the primary cause of pain in your life."

"You really think so?"

"No. I'm just messing with you."

"Daughters, diplomats, off your seat, swing each other to the beat."

"That's you."

"I'm off."

"Remember what I said about the Russian ambassador."

"Oh, Daddy—"